Leadership and Motivation in LEAN Times

A Handbook for Leaders in Government and Business

MARY T. MEYER

The author gratefully acknowledges the permission to use quotations or passages as indicated below.

The Leadership Style Assessment is from *Compendium of Questionnaires and Inventories Volume II,* by Sarah Cook. Copyright 2007. Used by permission of the publisher, HRD Press, Inc., Amherst, MA (800) 822-2801 www.hrdpress.com

Servant Leadership excerpts from the writings of Robert K. Greenleaf are reprinted by permission of the Greenleaf Center for Servant Leadership. Copyright Robert K. Greenleaf Center, Inc., 2008.

Celebrate What's Right with the World. Copyright MMX Dewitt Jones. No part of the content may be reproduced in any form, or by any means, unless written permission is granted from the publisher. Address all inquiries to Star Thrower Distribution: 800.242.3220, info@starthrower.com, www.DewittJones.com or www.Starthrower.com.

Leadership and Motivation in LEAN Times: A Handbook for Leaders in Government and Business by Mary T. Meyer. All rights reserved. No part of this book may be reproduced, stored in a retrieval system, or transmitted in any form or by any means without permission in writing from the author, except by a reviewer, who may quote briefly in review.

Edit, Design and Production by Lisa Latin http://lisalatin.com
Cover Image (c) 2009 Philip Anthony Decamotan, http://istock.com/Draco77

First edition, second printing, 2011
Second edition, 2014

Published in the United States of America.

For more information:
Mary T. Meyer
MTM Consulting, LLC
P.O. 12863
Salem, OR 97309
Author's Website: www.marytmeyer.com

ISBN-13: 978-1496017741

ISBN-10: 1496017749

DEDICATION

This book is dedicated to Mary Pearmine, former Marion County Commissioner, who was an exemplary leader with grace, compassion, political savvy, and a great sense of humor.

"No leader reaches big goals without the commitment, energy, dedication, and loyalty of a very strong and skilled staff."
—Barbara Roberts

ACKNOWLEDGMENTS

First of all, Laurie Steele, Treasurer for Marion County, introduced me to Stacey Crane at the Public Treasury Institute. Stacey was instrumental in elevating this content from a conference presentation to a leadership training manual, which then led to the creation of this book. These two people have provided guidance, encouragement, and document review along the way. In addition, Brenda Phillips, Ludie Arellano, Loren Maas, RickeyAnn Evans, Anne Baumgartner, Marita Meyer, Peggy Meyer, Alice Morton, and Matt Hornyak provided their time to review and edit the manuscript. I am grateful for their support, encouragement, wit and wisdom through this process.

Robin Rose is a local professional colleague and self-published author, who gave me hope throughout this process. She also connected me with my editor, Lisa Latin, who has been incredibly patient through numerous edits, and provided her expertise and professional guidance to this novice writer, as well as a delightful sense of humor. A friend recommended Candace Sinclair as a reputable publisher and someone who does marketing for new authors. Candace helped bring this book to the broader public, and converted it to an eBook and print book. She has been a trusted professional and wise mentor. In addition, Jean Trenary added her desktop publishing skills to polish and finalize the formatting of the manuscript, making it easier to upload to Amazon CreateSpace. Jean provided a new set of eyes for final formatting, new energy for the final stretch, patience and a sense of humor. It really takes a village and I am blessed to have had all these folks in the trenches and the minutiae to keep this book moving forward.

Several others provided inspiration and encouragement along the way: Claire lent visionary insights and positive affirmations; Bruce Blackstock Hazen guided me through the early stages of my career transition with such grace and expertise, finally helping me to realize my calling; my mother, Dorothy G. Meyer, who always emphasized the importance of correct spelling and grammar; and my Aunt Gertrude who was an exemplary English teacher and held us all to a high standard, even in writing occasional greeting cards. Most importantly, my ever-present divine guidance brought inspiration and perseverance throughout the creative writing process.

In addition, the insights shared in this book were gleaned from workshops, classes, participants, experiences, and conversations over the years. I have had the opportunity to work with many exemplary leaders, as well as a few who were actually demeaning and demotivating. I also worked with the line staff of these leaders and clearly observed the results of effective and ineffective leadership styles. My gratitude goes out to all of these people for the lessons learned, their time, dialogue, and support in bringing this project to fruition.

PURPOSE

This book was designed for leaders in government and industry—specifically: elected officials, department heads, managers, and supervisors.

In consideration of your valuable time, each topic is presented in brief summary format. When you find a subject that is of particular interest or pertinence to your current workplace challenges, references are provided so that you may delve deeper for more information. The scope of topics included is purposefully broad, in an attempt to address both current and potential future challenges related to leadership and motivation.

You will also find practical exercises, reflective questions, and personal applications—all designed to assist you when you make efficient theoretical concepts relevant in your workplace.

Though leadership is a quality that may be demonstrated by anyone at any level in an organization, the purpose of this book is to provide designated leaders with the awareness and skills needed to lead during challenging times.

It is important to know when to lead, and to be aware of the transitions between current and future states—these are the pivotal moments when employees look to their leaders for realistic direction and profound guidance.

Learning Objectives

When you have completed reading this book and have engaged in all or most of the practical exercises, you will be able to:

- Describe your leadership style during challenges and changes
- Explore several emerging leadership trends including Servant Leadership, Stewardship, LEAN Management, and Embracing Diversity
- Identify current issues in your team or organization
- Apply several strategies to motivate your employees
- Develop strategies to sustain momentum and resiliency
- Write and implement a short-term action plan to apply these concepts

Organization of Content

This book is written in a manner that invites you to be an active participant in learning and applying the concepts presented. Practical exercises (indicated by ▶) are included to assist you in applying the concepts. You will gain the most benefit if you dedicate some time to reflect on and engage in the exercises. There are also supplemental materials provided on the author's website at www.marytmeyer.com. Numerical footnotes reference additional information about source materials. Please see the corresponding Bibliography and References section for more information.

How to Use This Book

While writing this book, the author considered several types of audiences. See which of the following approaches work best for you.

Facilitated Workshops. The most ideal use of this book is as the primary training manual for a leadership workshop at your organization. To request more information about leadership workshops and train-the-trainer sessions, please contact the author through her website at www.marytmeyer.com.

Self-Study Manual. You'll quickly discover that the leadership and motivation sections are short, and you can read them over lunch or at your convenience. The Leadership Style Assessment found in the section on "What is Leadership?" under "Your Leadership Style," is essential to understanding the content that follows. Be sure to complete that assessment when you read the Leadership section.

Individual Coaching for Employees. You can use this book to coach your own employees as part of a professional development plan. If you have an employee who you want to promote to a leadership position, select the appropriate sections to review and discuss with the employee.

CONTENTS

Contents

CHAPTER 1

LEADERSHIP—CURRENT AND EMERGING TRENDS

In lean and challenging times, employees look to their leaders for guidance, behaviors, attitudes, and direction. Whether you know it or not, they are expecting you to pay attention to what's going on with them—their stress, morale, and performance—in response to decisions being made by the larger organization.

Key topics covered in this chapter:
- What is Leadership?
    - Leadership vs. Management
    - Principles of Leadership
    - Your Leadership Style
- Leadership in the Public Sector
- Emerging Trends in Leadership
    - Peer-to-Boss Transition
    - What is "LEAN" Management?
    - Leading at a Higher Level
    - Servant Leadership
    - Stewardship
- The Future of Leadership

Employee motivation truly starts with the leadership and environment created for the workers. So, we'll begin by talking about leadership and some behaviors and qualities that impact motivation.

What is Leadership?

In the last several years, we have seen such disillusionment with the role of leaders in major organizations. Many people are asking, "How can we turn things around?" and "How can we get compassion and ethics back into the workplace and not just focus on profits and the bottom line?" Others are asking, "What happened to managerial courage? Why doesn't my manager step up?"

Definitions are often a good place to begin. Here are some quotes from leading experts[1] on the topic of leadership:

- Warren Bennis: "Leadership is a function of knowing yourself, having a vision that is well communicated, building trust among colleagues, and taking effective action to realize your own leadership potential."

- Peter Drucker: "The only definition of a leader is someone who has followers."

- Don Clark: "Leadership is a process by which a person influences others to accomplish an objective and directs the organization in a way that makes it more cohesive and coherent." [This definition is similar to Northouse's definition, "Leadership is a process whereby an individual influences a group of individuals to achieve a common goal."]

- *Collins English Dictionary*: 1. The position or function of a leader; 2. The period during which a person occupies the position of leader: during her leadership very little was achieved; 3. a. the ability to lead. b. (as modifier): leadership qualities. 4. the leaders as a group of a party, union, etc.: the union leadership is now very reactionary.

▶ What is your definition of leadership?

▶ What are the qualities that you seek to model as a leader? (List 5-10 qualities.)

Leadership vs. Management

> "Over 50% of all professionals who hold management positions are still acting like individual contributors... An additional 25% of all managers are stuck between the roles of individual contributor and manager and seem unable to move fully into the Manager-Leader role."[2]

Before beginning this section, take a moment to reflect on your current way of thinking about leadership and management. You may discover some new information by the time you are done with this section.

What differentiates leadership from management? In his book, *On Becoming a Leader*, Warren Bennis said, "Managers are people who do things right, while leaders are people who do the right thing." Another frequent reference is that *managers have subordinates and leaders have partners.*

Though this book focuses on leadership, it is important to emphasize that to be successful, organizations need both effective leaders and effective managers.

The table below captures some of the characteristic distinctions between leaders and managers. (Source: www.changingminds.org[3])

SUBJECT	LEADER	MANAGER
Essence	Change	Stability
Focus	Leading people	Managing work
Have	Followers	Subordinates
Horizon	Long-term	Short-term
Seeks	Vision	Objectives
Approach	Sets direction	Plans detail
Decision	Facilitates	Makes
Power	Personal charisma	Formal authority
Appeal to	Heart	Head
Energy	Passion	Control
Culture	Shapes	Enacts
Dynamic	Proactive	Reactive
Persuasion	Sell	Tell
Style	Transformational	Transactional
Exchange	Excitement for work	Money for work
Wants	Achievement	Results
Risk	Takes	Minimizes
Rules	Breaks	Makes
Conflict	Uses	Avoids
Direction	New roads	Existing roads
Truth	Seeks	Establishes
Concern	What is right	Being right
Credit	Gives	Takes
Blame	Takes	Blames

▶ From your perspective, how is leadership different than management?

You have probably known some good managers who are not good leaders, and some good leaders who are not good managers—and perhaps a rare few who are both good leaders and good managers.

▶ Are you a leader, a manager, or both? Take another look at the previous table, and assess yourself. Place a check mark next to any qualities that you identify with, and then circle any that you feel are reflective of your particular strengths.

Have you ever noticed that effective leaders surround themselves with people whose skills complement their own? Think about the list of leadership characteristics (previously shown) and your own willingness to share leadership roles.

- Do you ask for input from your employees?
- Do you delegate meeting facilitation?
- Do you assign others to lead projects?
- Do you ask knowledgeable peers or staff to represent your department or program at public forums?
- Do you cultivate leadership in others?

When leaders surround themselves with competent people who have complementary skills, they naturally increase engagement, raise commitment levels, and make the best use of each employee's strengths.

Principles of Leadership

Stephen R. Covey is one of the most noted authors on the topic of leadership principles. In his book, *Principle-Centered Leadership*[4] Covey challenges us to:

- Look at why we do what we do.
- Identify the principles by which we lead.
- Create a personal mission statement.
- Keep our principles and priorities in front of us every day.

This approach supports leaders in remaining more true to themselves. Principle-centered leaders tend to stay on course with the direction they set for themselves and their organizations.

Are you aware of the principles by which you lead? In addition to Covey's book, this list of leadership principles from the U.S. Army[5] might be thought-provoking for you. [In the following list, each core principle is followed by my comments.]

The U.S. Army's Principles of Leadership

1. **Know yourself and seek self-improvement.** Assess your strengths, your leadership style, and your communication style. Develop self-awareness about how you respond to others and how you make decisions. Hire, collaborate, and delegate to complement your strengths, and be willing to learn about new concepts, systemic changes, and technologies.

2. **Be technically and tactically proficient.** Know your operation on a practical level. Employees have more respect for a manager who knows what they do, understands the processes and impacts, and makes informed decisions.

3. **Seek responsibility and take responsibility for your actions.** Step up in your department, management team, and community. Be accountable for your actions—no excuses, no blaming.

4. **Make sound and timely decisions.** Listen to all sides of an issue, receive input and collaborate toward sound decisions. Plan your work so you can submit a decision ahead of schedule or on time. Increase your ability to think on your feet when an immediate decision is required, and then stand by your decision.

5. **Set the example.** Your employees look to your words and behavior as the example to follow. Be aware of what you say and do, and how it impacts others. Be an example of the values and principles you teach and expect of others. Remember, people are watching what you do and don't do, what you say and don't say.

6. **Know your employees and look out for their welfare.** Take time to get to know your people as individuals—their interests, needs, and motivations. Let them know you care, and that you are watching out for their needs. Be there to support them in times of organizational challenges as well as personal crises.

7. **Keep your employees informed.** People need informational updates to be effective at their jobs. Help them by providing a heads-up about upcoming changes. Employees respect a manager or leader who operates with a "no surprises" philosophy. Likewise, managers and leaders appreciate employees who keep them informed about any pertinent issues, conversations, or concerns.

8. **Develop a sense of responsibility in your employees.** Set clear expectations around behaviors and task responsibilities, and then hold your people accountable. Build a sense of personal responsibility through teaching critical thinking skills, problem-solving, and decision making.

9. **Ensure that the task is understood, supervised, and accomplished.** Be responsible for the end result. Delegate clearly, allow clarifying questions, ask employees to summarize their understanding, and schedule progress checks. Provide oversight and coaching to bring a project to fruition on time and on budget.

10. **Build the team.** Be intentional about helping team members build their skills such that the team is cohesive, competent, loyal, and healthy. Set a clear strategic direction, goals and objectives, roles and responsibilities. Conduct productive meetings and facilitate dialogue to develop and update action plans. Reward and recognize efforts and accomplishments. Develop leadership within the team and support team members in moving toward self-management and career advancement.

11. **Employ your unit in accordance with its capabilities.** Assess individual and team strengths and weaknesses. Optimize each person's strengths and support them in developing new skills. Be strategic about complimenting an individual member's abilities and provide coaching to build competency and confidence.

As you read that list, were you in alignment with the principles? Are there others that you live by that are not on the US Army's list? Take a moment to reflect, identify, and write about *your* operating principles.

▶ My Leadership Principles

> *"Leadership is lifting a person's vision to higher sights, the raising of a person's performance to a higher standard, the building of a personality beyond its normal limitations."*
> —PETER F. DRUCKER

Your Leadership Style

Leadership styles change as society and workplaces evolve. Back in the day, it was quite common to adopt an autocratic style of leadership. Now, it is widely seen as being ineffective, and at times even archaic. The boss who says, *"My way or the highway"* or *"Don't think, just do what I say"* is fast becoming a dinosaur.

The same is true of the manager or leader who treats everyone too much the same. Often this approach is due to the leader's own lack of ability to be versatile or situationally appropriate.

Paul Hersey and Ken Blanchard introduced the concept of a *situational leader*[6] as one who can competently assess a situation and provide the appropriate level of intervention or support needed by the employees. They introduced four styles of leadership: telling, selling, supporting, and delegating. As well, they gave us four types of support that are needed for each situation.

To effectively intervene, Blanchard suggests that the leader must assess not only the situation but also the employee's level of competence and confidence. Ultimately, every leader needs to realize that it's not "one size fits all" with employees or peers. Individuals respond differently to different leadership styles.

So, knowing this, the question to ask yourself is: How can I be most effective in this situation with this person?

Leadership Style Assessment

In this section, you're presented with a leadership style assessment that is similar to Blanchard's model. It was developed by Sarah Cook[7] and is used by the North Carolina Office of State Personnel. It is included here because it is one of the best tools available for helping leaders develop greater self-awareness.

▶   Before you go any further, take the time to complete this Leadership Style self-assessment.

The information this assessment provides is critical to your best use and understanding of the information that's contained in the remainder of this book. Be sure to complete all four parts.

_____ Part 1: Self-assessment

_____ Part 2: Scoring

_____ Part 3: Identify your leadership style

_____ Part 4: Review the interpretation of typical behaviors

Leadership Style Self-Assessment: Part 1

This self-assessment profile will help you assess your preferred leadership style. Read the following descriptions and rate yourself on a scale from 1 to 5:

5 = I always do this.
4 = I often do this.
3 = I occasionally do this.
2 = I seldom do this.
1 = I never do this.

When interacting with my team members, I:

1. Have responsibility for problem solving and decision making.　　5　4　3　2　1

2. Give instructions and share information.　　5　4　3　2　1

3. Clarify work procedures and standards.　　5　4　3　2　1

4. Evaluate performance.　　5　4　3　2　1

5. Identify problems and develop action plans to resolve them.　　5　4　3　2　1

6. Create objectives for each person.　　5　4　3　2　1

7. Control decision making.　　5　4　3　2　1

8. Allocate resources.　　5　4　3　2　1

9. Provide direction.　　5　4　3　2　1

10. Ask for opinions and information.　　5　4　3　2　1

11. Coordinate what team members are doing, but not how they are doing it.　　5　4　3　2　1

12. Build trust in the team.　　5　4　3　2　1

13. Facilitate communication with and among others.　　5　4　3　2　1

14. Ask for and am receptive to ideas.　　5　4　3　2　1

15. Encourage participation.　　5　4　3　2　1

16. Reconcile difficulties when reported.　　5　4　3　2　1

17. Monitor performance directly.　　5　4　3　2　1

18. Focus on what the team members are feeling.　　5　4　3　2　1

19. Encourage a good team spirit.　　5　4　3　2　1

20. Show confidence in team members' abilities.　　5　4　3　2　1

Leadership Style Self-Assessment Scoring: Part 2

Total your rating for questions 1 to 10 from Part 1. These questions relate to task-related leadership behaviors—the horizontal axis in the graph below. These behaviors include telling people what to do, explaining, giving information, and directing.

Score for task-related behaviors (horizontal axis): _____

Now, total your rating for questions 11 to 20 from Part 1. These questions relate to people-related leadership behaviors—the vertical axis in the graph below. These behaviors include asking people for ideas, encouraging them, and building trust.

Score for people-related behaviors (vertical axis): _____

Plot your score on the graph below by putting an X where your rating for the horizontal axis and the vertical axis meet.

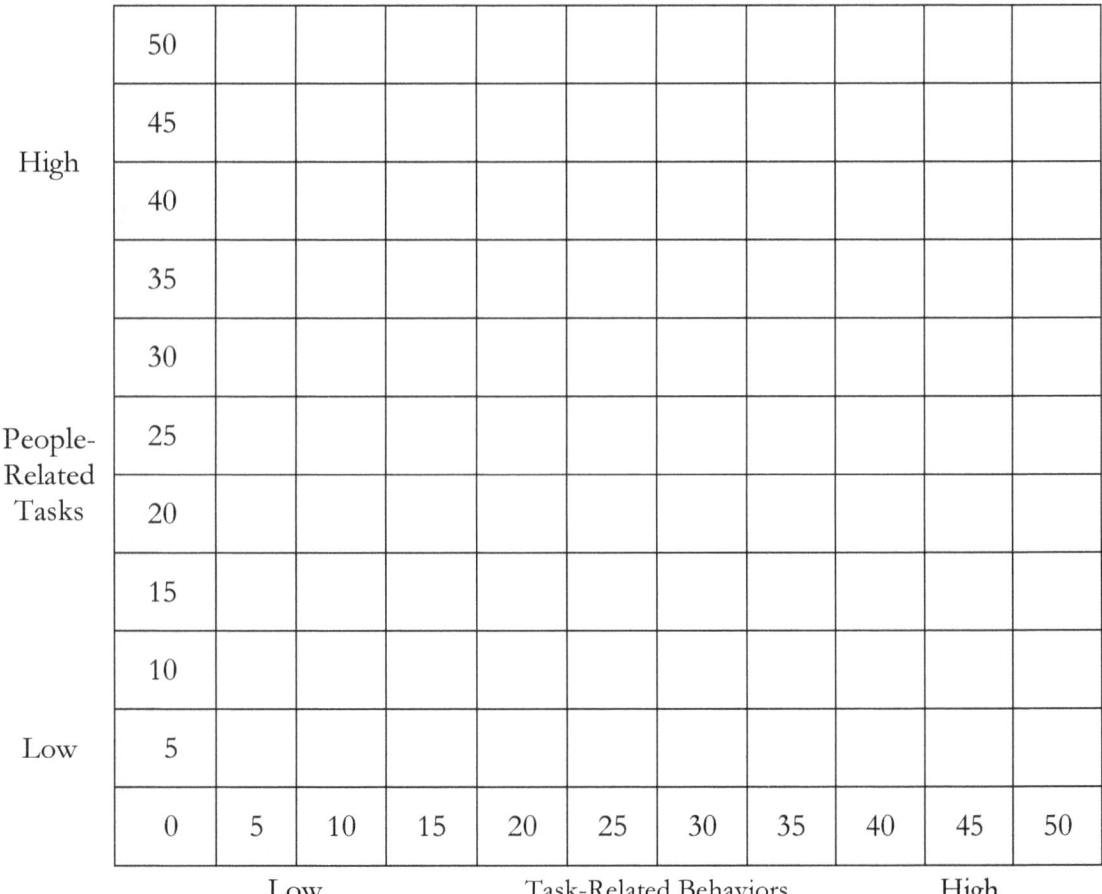

Compendium of Questionnaires and Inventories Volume II, by Sarah Cook, copyright © 2007. Used by permission of the publisher, HRD Press, Inc., Amherst, MA. (800) 822-2801; www.hrdpress.com.

Leadership Style Score Interpretation: Part 3

There are four possible leadership styles:

- Facilitating
- Guiding
- Empowering
- Directing

Look at the area on the graph where your two scores meet. Put an X or a dot at that location to indicate your score. This represents your leadership style.

		Facilitating					Guiding			
High	50									
	45									
	40									
	35									
	30									
People-Related Tasks	25									
	20									
	15		Empowering					Directing		
	10									
Low	5									
	0	5	10	15	20	25	30	35	40	45	50

Low   Task-Related Behaviors   High

Leadership Style Typical Behaviors: Part 4

	Facilitating	Guiding
High People- Related Tasks	Guides, listens, facilitates Encourages shared decision making and responsibility Monitors performance and is available for feedback	Combines instruction (telling) with asking questions Encourages feedback and contributions from team members Monitors performance and rewards positive behavior
	Empowering	**Directing**
Low	Clarifies and agrees on objectives with full participation of team members Gives support if requested Monitors indirectly, reconciles difficulties when reported	Gives clear and extensive instructions, along with training Is clear about expectations and procedures Rigorously monitors performance

Low	Task-Related Behaviors	High

Compendium of Questionnaires and Inventories Volume II, by Sarah Cook, copyright © 2007. Used by permission of the publisher, HRD Press, Inc., Amherst, MA. (800) 822-2801; www.hrdpress.com.

▶ According to this assessment tool, what is your primary leadership style?

So how does all this relate to your workplace? Can you imagine using the empowering style with a brand new employee? Or using the directing style with a long-term, high performing employee? That's probably not such a good idea. Both of these situations highlight the importance of maintaining self-awareness and assessing the level of confidence and competence of your employee. Leadership really is situational, isn't it?

► How will you use this Leadership Style information?

With Management Peers	With Employees
In Building Teams	**At Home**

Keep this information in mind as you continue your journey in the sections that follow. How does your leadership style affect the ways you act and react to various situations and challenges?

Leadership in the Public Sector

Clearly, there is a difference between public and private sectors. I have worked in training and development for over twenty years. Eighteen of those years involved working in the public sector, but I started my career in the for-profit private sector.

Following are several key differences I experienced when I transitioned from the private sector to public service:

- Public sector is not about profit and sales.
- Many agencies are sole providers.
- It is counter-culture to a global economy that focuses on choices for the customer. (Some agencies actually limit or take away choices for citizens.)
- Public officials are constantly under the scrutiny of citizens, regulatory agencies, and the media.
- Most of the services provided are mandated by law.

▶ How do these and other unique factors about working in government affect the way *you* lead *your* employees?

We have all heard the common refrain, "Government is different." While this may be true, there are many useful concepts and practices from the private sector, particularly in the realm of leadership that can and do apply to government agencies. After all, leadership is about people.

In recent years, I have talked with leaders at the National Guard, U.S. Postal Service, Internal Revenue Service, and Department of Human Services, who were all working on LEAN management, business process improvement, and empowering employees. I feel hopeful that many government leaders are already committed to a more efficient way of providing services.

When I hear about efforts toward sustainability and community partnerships, I believe a shift is happening *within* the public sector. It looks like many organizations are moving toward providing not just "mandated services" but the *right services* in the *right ways*.

I don't know that government will ever evolve beyond a bureaucratic structure, or that it would be appropriate to try. However, I do know that it's possible to be an effective leader within a bureaucratic structure, to share leadership, and to be respectful and inclusive of line staff. I challenge all leaders within bureaucratic systems to move beyond the traditional constraints of a bureaucracy and to think about how new leadership models might help government evolve and improve.

On the resources page of my website, you'll find a white paper, *Developing Leaders in the Public Sector.*[8] This article reviews some of the critical business issues, opportunities, threats, leadership issues, and information about developing leadership competencies. Research on the top concerns for public sector leaders today is highlighted. Also, it may provide you with ideas to consider as you review the next chapter in this book titled, "Workplace Issues and Challenges."

▶ Read "Developing Leaders in the Public Sector."

In addition to leadership development, one urgent concern of many public sector organizations today is succession planning. While elected officials and department heads cannot *guarantee* someone a job, there is much you can do to support those employees who are interested in, and committed to, developing leadership capabilities. You can ensure leadership and operational continuity during election or management transition times. You can motivate employees by providing acting-in-capacity or project management opportunities to assist them in getting the skills they need to advance.

You might also consider sharing this book as well as other training materials to help others develop their leadership capabilities.

Emerging Trends in Leadership

So far, we have discussed leadership definitions, principles, styles, and characteristics, and we've touched on public sector leadership. Now, let's move into *Emerging Trends in Leadership*. What's new, and where are we going?

Peer-to-Boss Transition

One of the critical issues in the workplace today is leadership retirement and continuity. Government is no exception.

Back in 1998, Marion County, Oregon, anticipated a massive wave of retirements and started a succession planning process. Between 1999 and 2009, they experienced more than 110 percent turnover in department heads, and approximately 80 percent turnover in managers and supervisors. That's a *huge* change for any organization! In addition, 60 percent of the line staff retired or moved on.

Inevitably, all this departure came with opportunities for internal promotions and new hires. What naturally follows is that the new managers realize they are now in charge of folks who used to be their peers. You can imagine the dilemmas that can result, and many of them do occur soon after the leadership change, especially if that change is not well managed.

The peer-to-boss transition can be successfully navigated if a few steps are followed in advance of the change, and a few shortly after the change.

1. Before the Change

Start training employees who want to get promoted or that you want to promote. Specifically, the following topics will help them succeed:

- Supervisory role
- Peer-to-boss transition

For some employees, getting the depth and complexity of the real job will help them self-select out of the recruitment process. For others, this will affirm that they are ready and willing to move forward.

Those who are ready to move forward should be approved to attend a series of management development classes to help them establish a solid foundation of the basics. Preferably, this training would be completed prior to obtaining the new leadership position.

2. After the Change

While orienting the new leader to his or her job responsibilities, be sure to also orient the other staff members and key contacts to the new leader. Clarify expectations right away: your expectations of them, their expectations of you, and their expectations of each other. This step is critical in raising awareness of past resentments that need to be let go, and any hopes that the new leader will be just like the beloved former leader. This is an opportunity to validate or invalidate expectations of the new leader and start with a clean slate.

Another key discussion for a new leader is to clarify roles and responsibilities. Some employees may have been doing extra duty while there was a staffing shortage due to the leadership transition. It's now time to provide relief for that extra workload and get people back to a realistic set of responsibilities. Or, this may be an opportunity to reconfigure how the tasks and duties are assigned. Then duties can be reallocated based on individual strengths and interests.

Once the new job is obtained, what can the new leader do to manage those former peer relationships? In her workbook, *Peer Today, Boss Tomorrow*,[9] author Laura E. Bernstein highlights four strategies to help new leaders navigate the changing role and to meet challenges that come with the new position:

1. Accept your leadership role and all that comes with it.
2. Set clear boundaries for all to follow.

This critical step helps new managers acknowledge their friendships inside and outside the workplace, and it helps them set clear roles and relationship boundaries with those folks (sooner than later) to prevent perceived or real favoritism from blossoming.

3. Communicate more effectively with everyone you lead.
4. Take action to get the results you want and need.

When we consider Peer-to-Boss transitions, we must also acknowledge that some public sector offices are quite small, perhaps having five or less employees. So, in order to seek a promotional opportunity, an employee may need to leave your department. Helping this employee prepare for promotion falls under "employee development." Whether employees stay in your group or not, you are still responsible for assisting in the development of their leadership skills.

Employees who know that their leaders support them in their growth and promotion are invigorated and trusting. They are more likely to request guidance and coaching, rather than just surprising you with their two weeks' notice. A supportive and development-oriented environment fosters employee willingness to *step up*.

In the current economic climate, we cannot guarantee people permanent employment, but we can assist their professional development and help them in becoming marketable whether they choose to move up or move on. Remember, how you treat people who leave has a great impact on the people who remain.

What is LEAN Management?

The State of Oregon Employment Department provides training on LEAN Management Basics,[10] including a clear and coherent summary of this widely-used approach to process improvement:

"LEAN Management is a series of methods by which an organization can become more efficient in the business processes used to provide services. By using these methods, a team or department can quickly implement ideas to reduce duplication, errors, or waste and to clarify or streamline processes resulting in improved turnaround times and increased customer satisfaction.

'LEAN' is a way of doing business focused on systematically and relentlessly eliminating waste in pursuit of 'True North'—highest quality, lowest cost, shortest lead time, best safety, and highest morale. LEAN initiatives have expanded as organizations have become more proactive in implementing changes necessary to allow them to survive and prosper in an ever-accelerating competitive environment.

LEAN focuses on valued-added processes and activities, defined as any activity that changes the way we do business or provide services that directly impacts our customers in a positive way, or in a way that they would willingly pay extra. Non-value-added activities should be eliminated, simplified, reduced, or integrated, whenever possible. Typically 95 percent of all lead time is non-value-added.

In eliminating waste, LEAN process analysis methods examine transportation, excess inventory, motion, waiting time, overproduction, over-processing, defects, and talent waste.

LEAN facilitators are trained to use Value Stream Mapping as a key tool in continuous improvement. Value Stream Mapping helps provide direction on what tools to use where, as well as determine the biggest causes and problems on which to focus first. A few components of continuous improvement include quick set-up, Kanban, Kaizen, flow, quality at the source, and 5-S. [For definitions, see the **LEAN Management Glossary** link on the Resources page on my website, www.marytmeyer.com.] The aim of LEAN Management is to increase standardized work, improve quality, and reduce variability in the process."

Here's an example of how this worked with one department:

A treasury department had a cumbersome deposit process involving duplication of effort in counting and handling the money. The process actually caused increased possibility of error, since it required three or four people to complete the procedure. In fact, the process was so cumbersome that there was only enough time to complete one bank deposit per week. Department customers complained. They needed *daily* deposits of their cash.

After taking time to analyze their workflow and getting more customer input, the treasury department redesigned their deposit process. The improvements now allow for employees to take turns counting money. One person verifies the count, and that is enough. The net result: the process was streamlined enough that they now make daily deposits, and they are meeting the needs of their customers!

"There is surely nothing quite so useless as doing efficiently
that which should not be done at all."
–PETER DRUCKER

▶ Can you think of areas in your workplace that could be improved through eliminating waste or increasing efficiency? If so, what are they?

▶ Can you think of areas where you or your employees could reduce errors or duplication of effort? If so, what are they?

▶ What can *you* do as a leader to engage your employees in these processes and ways of thinking?

LEAN Management provides tools for management and employees to streamline their processes. It is amazing how much time is wasted in organizations due to unclear processes, poorly maintained equipment, and uninformed people. One colleague of mine joked about her work environment, saying that they do teambuilding through repairing equipment malfunction and people dysfunction. She was frustrated that it took so much time to find and fix things each day that it did not leave them with enough time to get their essential work done.

When employees are able to come to work and do their job in an organized and predictable way, they are more productive and efficient. When leaders can help provide an environment for employees where processes are clearly identified and communicated, duplication is minimal, and errors are the exception. That results in the employees becoming better able to accomplish the task at hand.

Leading at a Higher Level

One of the leaders that inspired me was a director named Bridget. She was the most congruent person I'd ever met—her words matched her actions. She was authentic, honest, a great listener, knowledgeable, and bright. She also had a wonderful sense of humor. Later, when I became a manager, I aspired to emulate those same qualities.

▶ Have you ever known or worked with a leader who inspired you or had a positive impact on you? If so, what specifically did he or she say and do?

If you are now an elected official, director, manager, or supervisor, do you remember why you wanted to become one? Have you thought recently about who you really want to be in this role, and how you want to positively impact those around you? Or, are you just running as fast as you can to put out all the fires around you? Take a few minutes to think about this right now.

▶ What were you hoping to accomplish when you first assumed your role as a department head, manager, or supervisor?

▶ In what ways have you fulfilled those hopes?

▶ What are your truest intentions about how you want to interact with others around you on a daily basis?

Recently, I came across a book that gave me hope and touched my heart: *Leading at a Higher Level* by Ken Blanchard.[11] I've been a fan of Blanchard's writing ever since I read the *One Minute Manager*. He does extensive research, then simplifies the concepts. The net result is that he has created a positive and encouraging view of the future of management. I want to share his vision with you:

> *"Leading at a Higher Level is the process of achieving worthwhile results while acting with respect, care, and fairness for the well-being of all involved."*
> –KEN BLANCHARD

How does that sound to you? Do you think this is possible?

Blanchard believes that the future of leadership includes the following principles.

- Leading with intention (aware and effective leadership)   _____
- Doing the right thing (ethics)   _____
- Developing mutual trust and respect (relationships)   _____
- Operating a profitable and well-run organization (success)   _____
- Always growing, inquiring, and developing (learning)   _____

▶ On a scale of 1-10 [with 1 being ineffective and 10 being very effective], rate yourself on the leadership qualities listed above.

The concepts presented in *Leading at a Higher Level* remind us that it doesn't have to be either/or... profit *or* people, results *or* relationships. For today and the future, it really must be both!

Employees are not just *resources* or *liabilities* in the budget. They are *assets* of an organization. Employees are the ones who help reach the goals. They make change happen. It is surprising that there are still organizations and managers who haven't incorporated this concept into their attitude and behavior. *Leading at a Higher Level* asks each of us to step up to our next highest self in quality and relationship.

Along this line, two other leadership topics have become more popular in recent years: Servant Leadership and Stewardship.

> *"The essential truth I'm discovering right now is that when we are together, more becomes possible. When we are together, joy is available. We need to learn how to be together: that is the essential work of the servant-leader."*
>
> –Margaret Wheatley

Servant Leadership

Servant Leadership is a philosophy and practice that is being adopted more frequently in the business world today. It is a term that was coined by Robert K. Greenleaf[12] in an essay titled, *"The Servant as Leader,"* first published in 1970.

What is Servant Leadership?

"The servant-leader is servant first... It begins with the natural feeling that one wants to serve, to serve *first*. Then conscious choice brings one to aspire to lead. That person is sharply different from one who is *leader* first, perhaps because of the need to assuage an unusual power drive or to acquire material possessions. The leader-first and the servant-first are two extreme types. Between them there are shadings and blends that are part of the infinite variety of human nature.

The difference manifests itself in the care taken by the servant-first to make sure that other people's highest priority needs are being served. The best test, and difficult to administer, is to ask these questions:

- Do those served grow as persons?

- Do they, while being served, become healthier, wiser, freer, more autonomous, more likely themselves to become servants?

- What is the effect on the least privileged in society? Will they benefit or at least not be further deprived?"

In his second major essay, *"The Institution as Servant,"* Greenleaf articulated what is often called the "credo." He wrote:

"This is my thesis: caring for persons, the more able and the less able serving each other, is the rock upon which a good society is built. Whereas, until recently, caring was largely person to person, now most of it is mediated through institutions - often large, complex, powerful, impersonal; not always competent; sometimes corrupt. If a better society is to be built, one that is more just and more loving, one that provides greater creative opportunity for its people, then the most open course is to raise both the capacity to serve and the very performance as servant of existing major institutions by new regenerative forces operating within them."

According to management consultant, Robert Bacal:

"Servant leadership tells us that leadership is collaborative and cooperative, and those that follow consent to be led, and cannot easily be coerced into following, particularly over the long haul. Building trust, using empathy, listening to and being responsive to followers and the ethical use of power are cornerstones of servant leadership."[13]

Servant Leadership excerpts from the writings of Robert K. Greenleaf are reprinted by permission of the Greenleaf Center for Servant Leadership. © Copyright Robert K. Greenleaf Center, Inc. 2008.

▶ As an elected official or public employee, have you heard the term "public servant?" Do you see this differently than servant leadership? If so, how?

▶ What are some ways in which you can demonstrate servant leadership in your relationships with employees, executives, and the community?

Stewardship

Another area of interest related to leadership in the public sector is the concept of stewardship. Public officials have long been expected to be good stewards of public funds and stewards of public trust.

▶ What does stewardship mean to you? How do you ensure stewardship in your role?

Peter Block wrote *Stewardship: Choosing Service Over Self-Interest.*[14] He was instrumental in bringing this concept and practice alive again.

Block says, "Stewardship is for everyone who is tired of bouncing from one improvement program to another while recognizing that the underlying forces of bureaucracy, self-interest, and control remain unchanged."

His key point is that choosing service over self-interest will result in deep organizational change and redistribution of power, purpose, and wealth. Instead of the control and regulation paradigm, stewardship extends partnership to employees and customers, which results in greater accountability and responsibility, and less of the old entitlement mentality.

▶ What are the areas of outdated bureaucracy, self-interest, dependency, and control in your workplace?

▶ What are some ways in which you can replace these outdated modes of operating with increased responsibility and partnership in your workplace?

The Future of Leadership

Where are we headed in the next ten to twenty years? Change is inevitable, but what will be different?

▶ What is *your* vision of the future? How do you see leadership developing in new ways? What behaviors and qualities would *you* like to see leaders demonstrate?

"The best way to predict the future is to invent it."
–ALAN KAY, noted computer scientist

Among the many resources on this topic, there are a number of common themes worth mentioning:

1. Leading with passion to inspire trust across cultures and generations. When cultures collide, taking a serving approach has a much higher chance of bridging the gap between cultures than does a relationship built on winning a power struggle. The servant-leader works from a position of reconciliation and seeks solutions that bridge differences and builds on the unique qualities of each stakeholder.[15]

2. Empowering employees by helping to build confidence and self-esteem, developing marketable skills, and coaching them to set their own goals.[16]

3. Encouraging employees to focus on one activity at a time. Multitasking has been proven to be non-efficient and is a loss of positive energy.[17]

4. Leadership competencies will still matter. There is a move away from viewing leadership and leadership development solely in terms of leader attributes, skills, and traits. Instead, the new approach involves seeing development as focusing on the whole person, the leader's ability to communicate, and his or her relationships and interactions as both a leader and collaborator with other staff.[18]

5. Implementing social responsibility programs at work and individual levels.[19]

6. The role of technology—leaders will be required to become more knowledgeable and competent with technological tools and be able to lead geographically dispersed units and teams. [20]

"The US cannot maintain its economic leadership unless our work force consists of people
who have the knowledge and skills needed to drive innovation."
–BILL GATES

7. Increasing interest in the integrity and character of leaders—the interrelationships between leadership, character and values will become more central to how leaders work. Issues such as integrity, moral character, ethical business practices, trustworthiness, humility, concern for the greater good, and fairness will increasingly be included in leadership development practices.[21]

8. Staying on top of the trends by listening to the grassroots people and also listening to the rebels.[22]

9. Maintaining the willingness and a strategy to make a right turn at a moment's notice. The pace of change is not slowing down.[23]

10. Shifting power, control and wealth. Several predictions include the crumbling of larger structures including financial institutions and governments, and the creation of newer, more equitable systems, with equal access to education, healthcare, jobs, and leadership. *The World is Flat* by Thomas Friedman raises provocative questions about how the development of smaller and third world countries is already impacting the power structures and global influence in ways that have nothing to do with who has the most money or the biggest weapons.[24]

11. Returning to Right Mindedness.

> *"In right-brain integrated societies, there is egalitarianism, rather than one gender holding power over the other. The worldview is holistic and oriented in the embodied rather than the abstract. These cultures value community, creativity, nurturing, empathy, intuitive intelligence, earth, nature, dreams, metaphor, poetry, art, connection, interdependence and synthesis. The orientation of time is not linear, but is cyclical and aligned with the eternal cycles of birth, growth, death and renewal."*
>
> –DALE ALLEN, IN OUR RIGHT MINDS[25]

Right Mindedness is an approach for balance, not swinging the pendulum to the other extreme, not either/or. It empowers the feminine while embracing and integrating the masculine.

▶ What steps will *you* take to start creating and moving toward *your* vision of the future?

Leadership Summary

This brings the leadership section to a close. In summary, you've learned about the following topics:

- What is Leadership?
    - Leadership vs. Management
    - Principles of Leadership
    - Your Leadership Style
- Leadership in the Public Sector
- Emerging Trends in Leadership
    - Peer-to-Boss Transition
    - What is "LEAN" Management?
    - Leading at a Higher Level
    - Servant Leadership
    - Stewardship
- The Future of Leadership

Following are a few key points from this section:

- Know yourself. Be honest about your style, strengths and weaknesses. If you want to know what you can do to motivate your people during lean times, start with yourself!

- Know your people. Learn their style, strengths, weaknesses, priorities, and motivators.

- Be your authentic self. Life is too short to pretend to be something you are not. If you are not cut out to be an effective leader, step down, or at least share the responsibilities with others who complement your talents.

- Treat people with respect. Everyone has value, regardless of their title.

If things aren't going well, you can do something about it. Step up into your leadership role and lead forward in a new direction. Leadership involves so many gifts and abilities, but they can be summarized by the four C's: Communication, Collaboration, Confidence, and Competence.

▶ Before we move forward, pause and reflect for a moment. Are there any questions you have at this point?

▶ Are there any topics that you would like to explore further?

▶ If you have not finished all of the self-reflective activities and the Leadership Style Assessment, go back and complete them before you continue to the next chapter.

CHAPTER 2

WORKPLACE ISSUES AND CHALLENGES

Uncertainty creates the conditions necessary for leadership.
–KOUZES & POZNER

▶ What issues and challenges are you aware of or experiencing in your work environment?

Here are some of the challenges other leadership workshop participants have experienced:

- Economy
- Budget cuts
- Layoffs/unemployment
- Declining productivity
- Leadership changes
- Interpersonal conflict
- War/global conflicts
- Challenging/angry customers
- Values or ethical conflict
- Nature of the work—collections, law enforcement
- Diversity—bilingual staff, immigration issues
- Generational differences
- Disagreement with decisions made
- Not having a service attitude

▶ Look at your list and the list above. Choose two challenges that will be your top priorities to focus on for the remainder of this book.

1. _____

2. _____

▶ Write down your initial thoughts as to some possible strategies to help address these two priorities. These may be things you have already tried but need to try again, or they may be things you have thought about doing but haven't yet tried.

Challenge #1:

Challenge #2:

It's a given that we all have challenges and many of them are outside of our control. One leadership lesson is to focus on what it is we can control and move forward on those things. This approach helps build confidence that we can resolve issues. When we experience success frequently, even if it comes in small doses, we naturally build momentum. This is true for everyone—leaders, managers, and employees alike.

When leaders and managers focus only on the final destination (and fail to acknowledge the small successes along the way), employees often become disengaged. They may even lose their commitment to the project or belief that it will ever come to completion.

Conversely, when you set milestones and acknowledge when they are met, you can track forward progress and team members can experience success, which helps everyone sustain momentum. It is important to celebrate milestones along the way, not only at the end destination. This helps employees feel appreciated, hopeful, and recharged. Consequently, they are likely to be in a better position to feel confident about moving forward to handle the next section of the project.

▶ What can you do to foster the opportunity for your employees to have small, frequent successes this week?

Another aspect of leading and managing in challenging times is contextual. The environment at large has a much higher level of stress and uncertainty. Your employees are impacted by this—both at work and at home.

You may already be asking yourself, "How can I keep my employees more productive?" or "How can I ensure that employees stay well and show up for work, so that we can stay productive as a team?"

There is another question you might also want to ask: "How can I motivate my employees during stressful and uncertain times, without a pay raise?"

In the chapters that follow, we will focus on strategies and tools that you as a leader can use to help your employees stay motivated and engaged even when times are challenging, the future is uncertain, pay raises are nowhere on the horizon, layoffs are looming, and staffing is lean.

"A kite flies highest not with the wind but against it."
–Winston Churchill

CHAPTER 3

HOW TO KEEP EMPLOYEES MOTIVATED

Key topics covered in this chapter:
- What is Motivation?
- Positive Recognition
- Non-Defensive Communication
- Leading Through Change

How do you stay motivated? How do you keep your employees motivated? When times get tough, these concerns are raised, often. Supervisors and managers want to know what they can do to improve morale, initiative, and motivation *without spending more budget dollars.*

In this chapter, you'll learn how to keep your employees motivated and productive, so they can accomplish the goals you've set for them.

> *"Leaders must be close enough to relate to others,*
> *but far enough ahead to motivate them."*
> –JOHN MAXWELL

What is Motivation?

One of the biggest differences between managers and leaders is the way they motivate people. Their style sets the tone for the events and future outcome of every project.

Motivation: "Leaders influence others to reach goals through their approaches to motivation. They can use either positive or negative motivation. A positive style uses praise, recognition, and rewards, and increases employee security and responsibility. A negative style uses punishment, penalties, potential job loss, suspension, threats, and reprimands."[26]

▶ What are you currently doing to help motivate your employees?

▶ What else could you try?

In Chapter 1, I told you about Bridget, a leader who inspired me. At one point, our organization had gone through several large system changes simultaneously. One of the things that made Bridget stand out was that she was attentive to the process. Every morning, her first priority was to touch base with her employees. At the end of the day, she followed up and thanked us for all the extra effort! It meant a lot to us that someone cared and noticed; that type of attentiveness is free. It doesn't require line item additions or creating and monitoring committees. No additional budget is required.

Managers can sometimes get so consumed by all the details of implementing changes that they forget to pay attention to their employees. I once coached a manager who actually said, "Well, the staff just has to deal with it." While that may be true in one sense, I noticed that this particular manager's approach wasn't working very well for the people he managed.

After a few weeks, his team was floundering. His comments also impacted me. I lowered my expectations of him as a manager and sought others to provide support or coaching. His comments and hands-off attitude told me that he was not a manager who saw himself as a change agent or leader.

▶ How about you? What is your natural tendency during challenging times?

▶ What do you do most often in your role as a manager: Do you close your office door, or do you get away from your desk and directly interact with your employees?

▶ Do you believe in recognizing people for doing well during challenging times? Or, do you wait until they do something "over and above" the norm?

Throughout this chapter on motivation, think about how your behavior, attitude, and decisions impact your employees. Think about how you enhance or discourage your employees' level of motivation.

"Leaders conceive and articulate goals that lift people out of their petty preoccupations and unite them in pursuit of objectives worthy of their best efforts."
–John Gardner

Positive Recognition

Where do you want to spend your time? Do you want to impose discipline, or do you want to provide recognition and appreciation?

Will recognition eliminate the need for discipline? In many cases, yes, but not always. However, recognition *will* significantly reduce the need for discipline. Remember, what gets rewarded gets continued. Are you aware of how you are rewarding the behavior of others through your behavior, time, and attention?

Think about the percentage of *your* time spent focused on what employees do well versus what they do wrong or incompletely. If you are not using positive feedback and recognition every day, you are missing a vital component of your role as a leader.

Ken Blanchard said, "Catch them doing something right." Try it and see how your focus changes over time.

Positive recognition is something you can start *now* that will help improve employee morale, re-engage distant employees, and create a more pleasant work environment. And it's FREE!

When I suggest that leaders and managers try to engage their employees through positive recognition, I often hear this resistant response: "Won't people think I'm a phony if I start praising them?"

It's an understandable concern, especially if you don't have much of a track record for rewarding employees with positive recognition. However, building a bridge is easier than you may think.

Try using a genuine bridging comment, such as, "I know this is long overdue, but I really want you to know how much I appreciate…"

Or, try this method one supervisor used. He found a cartoon about a crabby manager and shared it with his employees by saying, "This cartoon reminded me of my behavior recently. I don't want to be like that. So, I want you to know that I'm going to try some different things, like positive feedback. Let me know how I'm doing after a couple weeks."

Most people respect that kind of honesty and appreciate the effort you're willing to make to evoke positive changes.

Giving more positive feedback and recognition might seem awkward at first, but after a while, it becomes more natural. It could make you wonder why you waited so long. Be specific. Tell your employee exactly what he or she did that resulted in you saying, "Good job!"

▶ Give three examples of how you could give positive feedback and recognition to an employee? (Be specific.)

1.

2.

3.

Create Events that Celebrate Your Employees

A fun way to recognize your employees is to celebrate together. This can include birthdays and personal events, as well as professional and team accomplishments.

I remember talking with one department head about an upcoming planning retreat, and I asked, "What did you do the last time to celebrate someone's accomplishments?"

He paused and said, "I can't remember ever doing that."

Make a point of celebrating accomplishments quarterly (or at the very least, once a year) to sustain momentum.

If you're experiencing challenges with morale, productivity, too much change, or disengaged employees, then positive feedback and recognition can produce a quick turnaround for getting employees back on track.

Celebrate What's Right with the World

One of my favorite inspirational films is by Dewitt Jones, *Celebrate What's Right with the World*.[27] Dewitt is a National Geographic photographer, and the film is filled with his beautiful pictures from around the world. The key concepts he shares can help leaders create a work environment in which their employees can thrive, rather than just survive. Plus, they help employees take ownership of their own attitudes and motivation. Several managers I know have used this film, or something similar, at their annual staff planning retreat. Celebrating is food for the spirit, and it's also a nice reminder about what's really important.

Key Concepts: Celebrate What's Right With The World

1. Believe it and you'll see it.
   - Commit to the results you're looking for.
   - Find ways around obstacles.
   - Have high expectations.

2. Recognize abundance.
   - Acknowledge all that you have to work with.
   - Broaden your definition of winning.
   - Look for ways to work cooperatively with others.

3. Look for possibilities.
   - Focus on opportunity, rather than scarcity.
   - Find what's working.
   - Keep looking for the next possible answer.

4. Unleash your energy to fix what's wrong.
   - Connect with a positive vision.
   - Believe that solutions exist.
   - Focus on what is right with the situation.

5. Ride the changes.
   - Realize that change is possibility.
   - Learn to live with uncertainty, yet act with confidence.
   - Challenge the order in your life.

6. Take yourself to the edge.
   - Trust yourself and create your own future.
   - Follow your edge wherever it goes.
   - Move beyond your best.

7. Be your best for the world.
   - Act with service and grace.
   - Make a contribution through action.
   - Talk about your successes to discover your dreams.

▶ How do you see yourself or your team applying these concepts in your workplace?

Non-Defensive Communication

In most organizations, employees are somewhat intimidated by their boss. In government, this seems to be escalated by the stronger policies, politics, unions, and increased security measures that are often present in a governmental environment. In my experience, and at the risk of over-generalizing, the lack of feedback coupled with conflict avoidance is more prevalent in government organizations than in private industry.

For example, even while law enforcement officers learn interpersonal skills to improve their work with the general public, not all of them transfer the knowledge and apply the skills with their coworkers and management peers. The problem is not restricted to any single group or industry. It's a problem across the board. The Bureau of Labor and Industries reported a 35 percent increase in claims regarding bullying and harassment from coworkers in all industries (1995-2005). Clearly, people still need help communicating safely with one another.

However, progress is also occurring. There is a movement spreading across the world that has had a very beneficial impact for both individuals and organizations: Non-Defensive Communication (also known as Nonviolent Communication, as taught and advocated by Marshall Rosenberg, Ph.D.). Non-Defensive Communication is a powerful concept that looks more deeply at how we give and receive feedback.

In this approach, the basic skills of active listening, giving feedback, clarifying, and summarizing are used. Communicating non-defensively also includes examining your intent, engaging empathy in the expression of your requests, and remaining open and neutral (for example, non-reactive) when receiving feedback. Some organizations offer training in a similar skill set called Appreciative Inquiry.

Now, just for a moment, think about the executives you work with, as well as the managers you have worked with in the past.

- Can you imagine some of those more intimidating executives suddenly becoming more caring in the way they listen to you?
- Can you imagine them actually listening, really listening, to your concerns?
- Can you see them validating your comments instead of being dismissive?
- Can you imagine them asking what kind of support they can offer?

What a difference this would make in any work environment! The benefits are not restricted to the workplace. Non-Defensive Communication has been effectively applied to improve relationships in a broad array of settings. People apply Non-Defensive Communication in all arenas: at home, in schools, volunteer groups, civic organizations, and spiritual communities, to name just a few.

► On a scale of 1-10 (1=low, 10=high), how comfortable are you with…

- Receiving feedback in general   _____

- Receiving feedback from your peers   _____

- Receiving feedback from your employees   _____

- Receiving feedback from your spouse/partner   _____

► What causes discomfort or anxiety about receiving feedback?

For you…

For your employees…

Communicating non-defensively is based on the principle that effective communication can happen when there is positive intent, a framework for the discussion, and follow-through. This one leadership change alone can significantly, constructively, and quickly shift the entire work culture.

How Does It Work?

First, you need to examine your own thoughts and feelings about the situation and the person, and be honest about what your part of the situation is: how have you allowed it to continue, have you ignored it, over-reacted, etc.?

Next, there are six steps to Non-Defensive Communication. It helps to think about these before starting the conversation with another person.

1. State your observation. What's going on? What is someone doing or saying?
2. Express how you are feeling in response to your observation.
3. Identify your underlying needs and intention.
4. Make your request(s) of the other person (words or behaviors to be changed).
5. Listen to the other person.
6. Make an agreement and set a date to follow through.

Here's an example of Non-Defensive Communication in action. It is drawn from a true story, but the names have been changed.

Sally was trying to apply Non-Defensive Communication in her interactions with her coworker, Ralph. They had a history of being unable to resolve issues together, and she sensed an underlying friction and frustration from him. When Sally approached Ralph to try to problem-solve the issues, he usually responded, "There's not a problem. It's your problem." Then he would walk away.

Sally asked her supervisor for help, and the supervisor contacted me to help facilitate a solution. The supervisor approached Sally and Ralph and requested they participate in a facilitated process using Non-Defensive Communication. When they realized that their supervisor's other option was to start a progressive discipline process on both of them, they agreed to try the facilitated process.

The supervisor asked if I would facilitate the meeting with Sally and Ralph, and I agreed. Prior to the meeting, I sent both of them the Six Steps to Non-Defensive Communication so they could each reflect on the situation and prepare their thoughts.

They came prepared and we generated some guidelines for the session related to being respectful of one another. I proposed that they commit from the start to stay present through to the resolution of the issues, and not abandon the process. After some clarifying discussion, both agreed.

Sally started by sharing her thoughts on steps 1-4: Observations, Feelings, Needs, and Request(s). I allowed Ralph to ask clarifying questions, but not to debate or discuss what was said. This part of the process allows for validation of each individual's perspective, without questions or diminishing remarks.

Then we switched to Ralph's comments on steps 1-4. At that point, both participants had listened to the other person (step 5), so we began to work on step 6: clarifying and prioritizing the concerns, and then examining the requests for reasonableness and feasibility.

In a two-hour session, Sally and Ralph had made four agreements that they felt they could commit to and implement within the first two weeks.

While we didn't get *all* the issues resolved in that first session, it was quite apparent that the friction had significantly been de-escalated. Sally felt "heard" and Ralph did own-up to his part of the dynamic. We followed up with progress check meetings over the next thirty, sixty, and ninety days to ensure stability of the new commitments. We also were able to address several other issues during those progress check sessions.

Following the process, I met with Sally and Ralph's supervisor. The end result, according to the supervisor, was that both Sally and Ralph had become more respectful, collaborative, and productive within a reasonable amount of time. The supervisor became curious about what I did to help them break through their animosity. I provided her with coaching on the process and facilitative techniques to assist with any future issues that may arise. This led to more extensive training for supervisors in several departments, because the process was viewed as delivering expedient and productive results.

The more you practice this model (and yes, it does take practice), the more productive and satisfying your communications will become—for you and for everyone you work with. Over time, people who use Non-Defensive Communication experience an uptick in other people's willingness to engage. Isn't it amazing what creating a safer environment will do for a person or a team?

The more you demonstrate and reinforce that communicating with you is safe, and that your team can communicate without getting defensive, the more people will feel safe to discuss and address issues. You'll be in a good position to have effective and productive dialogue.

In addition, the following two key points are known for making this approach successful:

- Be prepared to focus your attention on the conversation. Do not allow interruptions.
- Get comfortable with silence. Give the other person time to think about how he or she wants to respond, without jumping in.

▶ Now it's your turn to practice the first four steps of Non-Defensive Communication. Think about a situation at work in which an employee or peer is behaving defensively with you or with one another. Describe your:

1. Observations

2. Feelings

3. Needs and Intention

4. Request(s)

▶ What are your thoughts about how the other person might respond to your comments and requests?

▶ How would you respond to their response?

▶ Would you be willing to be flexible if the other person's response is not what you expected? What if they surprise you (pleasantly or unpleasantly)?

▶ What would stop you from going to that person and having this conversation right now?

Your ability to answer these questions honestly will strengthen your capacity to be non-defensive and will proactively address any vulnerability you may feel. Whether you are aware of it or not, most people feel vulnerable about the possibility of unexpected behaviors or an unpredictable outcome when they actually experience this type of conversation.

When confronted with a situation or behavior that you know needs to change, ask yourself: Why is this allowed to continue happening? Why am I allowing this to continue?

You can only be as honest with others as you are with yourself. Exploring your own vulnerability will help you feel more confident and safe about engaging with the conversation. It helps break up patterns of avoidance. Conversely, when you ignore or deny your feelings of vulnerability, you tend to stay locked into long-term patterns of conflict avoidance.

▶ Are you willing to commit to having this conversation within the next week?

CHAPTER 4

LEADING THROUGH CHANGE

We are living in times of non-stop, large-scale change, and it's all happening simultaneously.

To lead others through change, it's important to first identify and manage your own response to the changes: how you feel about it, whether or not you agree with the decisions being made, how it will impact you and your employees, and the benefits to you and your customers.

More often than not, there is very little time to complete this personal assessment before your employees start asking questions. Their responses to the changes require you to step into the leadership role proactively. It becomes your responsibility to help guide them in a strategic manner to get from here to there. It's your job to lead the transition.

There are six typical responses to change:[28]

1. Enthusiasm
2. Initiative
3. Confusion
4. Anger
5. Withdrawal
6. Loss of identity

For each of these responses, you may observe behaviors and emotions that require an appropriate and situational response from you. For example, the confused employee may need information, while the withdrawn employee may need support and encouragement. Employees with initiative will need tasks delegated to foster their willingness to move things forward. For more information, refer to "*What Happens to People During Transition*" on the Resources page of the www.marytmeyer.com website.

In addition to the responses to change, three stages of personal transition were introduced by William Bridges[29] - the ending, the neutral zone, and the new beginning. For each of these stages, the leadership role is critical in moving people forward successfully.

- **Endings**. Listen to the comments about loss and help bring closure to what is ending. As things change, continue to honor the people who are letting go of what they helped create. As much as possible, give a clear vision of the new beginning to help build recognition of how the change will look different than current processes, behaviors, or policies.

- **Neutral Zone**. Patiently answer the questions about why, what, when, how, and who. Tell employees what you *do* know as well as what is *not* changing. This will help keep a solid foundation under their feet so they can keep moving forward.
- **New Beginnings**. Celebration and recognition are important, in addition to a more clear definition of the new policy, processes, roles, or behaviors.

▶ What is your tendency when responding to change? Do you embrace change or do you avoid it?

▶ How do you communicate with people about the upcoming changes? How inclusive are you?

▶ When is it important to communicate with others? At what stages?

▶ Do you tell your employees the "what-why-when-who and how," or do you expect them to just willingly jump on board?

To most effectively manage transitions, William Bridges has developed a model with 5 Steps to Implement Change:[30]

1. Preparation
2. Planning
3. Transition Measures
4. Implementation
5. Celebration

The unique factor about this model is the recommendation that key constituents be involved from the beginning, including line staff employees. The "end user" will bring up essential questions in the planning stage to assist with a more informed process and implementation.

Another unique aspect of this model is the use of Transition Measures. This step creates support mechanisms, processes, and policies during the transition period. These may have an end date (sunset period) once the change is completed. Transition measures help people avoid the "wait and see" mentality.

In their book, *The Leadership Challenge*,[31] Kouzes and Pozner discuss leadership excellence in uncertain times. They mention two prerequisites for guiding people through turbulent waters:

1. *Hardiness* for mastering risk and the challenge of change
2. *The ability to make decisions* under conditions of extreme uncertainty

First, let's look at the concept of *hardiness*. How can a leader or manager create an environment that generates hardiness? Kouzes and Pozner recommend that leaders foster "a sense of commitment, control and challenge if people are to feel healthy and hardy as they participate in innovations that have an effect on their work lives."

A critical element of hardiness is the belief that the result of the new change is worthy of their best efforts. People need to know that they are "dedicating themselves to the creation of a noble and meaningful future." This is so important!

It is difficult to measure or quantify how much initiative has been lost through poorly planned or executed change efforts. How many times have you dedicated yourself to a project you felt was meaningful, only to have it abandoned midstream? How do *you* manage the need to follow through when implementing a project while also being responsive to changes in customer needs?

Other synonyms for hardiness include endurance, self-assurance, stamina, and durability. These are all critical qualities for thriving amidst continuous change, and indeed, lean times do generate continuous change.

Leading people through change can be challenging, but it's also an opportunity to innovate. In the midst of change, when it feels like the walls are coming down around you, that is the time of heightened creativity, a time for venturing outside the constraints of the way it always was.

Kouzes and Pozner wrote about this quite eloquently:

> "Their [the leader's] first act during times of adversity is to create a climate in which organizational members can also accept the challenge of change. To create purposeful movement out of uncertainty, leaders must also guide and channel the often frenetic human motion of change toward some end. When things seem to be falling apart, leaders must show us the exciting new world we can create from the pieces. Out of the uncertainty and chaos of change, leaders rise up and articulate a new image of the future that pulls the organization together."[32]

Now, let's look at the second prerequisite: *the ability to make decisions during conditions of extreme uncertainty*.

What are your concerns about making decisions in uncertain times? Why is decision making during lean times different than decision making during more certain times?

Fundamentally, making decisions in uncertain times is not that different from decision making in certain times. The decision-making process is similar, but has a shorter time frame and a greater sense of urgency.

This urgency can bring with it a sense of fear of not having all the information to make a sound decision. At the core of this fear is the fear of making the wrong decision. Today, the risks are more global, and the impacts are deeper and broader. A leader's credibility may also be at risk. A decision made today may need to change tomorrow, given new information. This change may result in an increase or a decrease in employee or customer trust in the decision maker.

Another concern is being out-of-the-loop about other upcoming changes that could derail your recent decision to implement something new. Staying in the communication loop is essential. Whether during project management or while planning a change, the unknown and unpredictable are variables outside your control. Finding out sooner about upcoming changes will help with a quicker course correction. However, there will be those times that you just have to do the best you can with what you have. You will have to move forward anyway.

You might need to surrender to the fact that you can't please everyone all the time. The decision you make in a time of urgency or uncertainty is one based on your expertise, experience, gut-feeling, and authority. While it may be a short-term solution, you may not have time to gather input from others or to build consensus in your team. Once the urgent situation has been addressed, there may be an opportunity to debrief with key people and to examine what went well, what could have been done differently/better, and what else needs to happen now.

Strategies for Making Effective Decisions in Extremely Uncertain Times

Managing through times of extreme uncertainty is the essence of "managing transition." Here's a list of five strategies to get you thinking about what might apply in your workplace:

Perspective

- Breathe deeply and regularly.
- Balance head and heart. It's not either/or; it's both.
- Expand your boundaries. Be constantly aware of the internal and external environment.
- Create an environment of innovation and creativity where best efforts and good tries are rewarded and mistakes are a tool for learning. That's when decision making in "shifting sands" becomes a way of life.
- Spend time with visionary people. See a broader view and get perspective.

Planning

- Assess the risks, regularly: the risk of doing/saying something, and the risk of doing/saying nothing.

- Build commitment before the decision and implementation begin. Involve all levels of constituents in the process of planning.

- Learn how to make sound decisions. Gather and analyze data from a variety of sources, develop criteria and parameters, invite collaboration, select the most feasible options, and make the decision.

- If you have very little time to make a decision, assess the risks and consequences, breathe deeply, and trust your gut and your intuition. Then make the decision and move forward.

- Be strategic in planning forward and also develop contingency plans. Stay in control of the things that are known and anticipate possible challenges. Establish an emergency management plan and process. When the unexpected happens, take time to deal with it.

People

- Tell your people what you do know, and tell them what is not changing. Over-communicate and manage the rumors.

- Communicate a clear vision of where you are going. Gain commitment to that vision from all employees, especially the resistant ones. The long-term vision helps carry people forward when short-term goals and strategies change to address immediate needs. That bigger picture still holds true, and it holds people together; they have a common purpose.

- Know your team of experts. If you don't have one, build one. Rely on your experts to keep you apprised of what's going on, what's changing, and decisions being made that might impact you or your department.

- If you have decided to just "wait it out," tell your people that. Don't leave them hanging and risk losing their trust in your ability to take action.

Personal

- Own it! Employees know that "you get paid the big bucks" because it's your responsibility to make tough decisions. Step up!

- Seek help sooner [ASAP] to get through the endings and neutral zone. It's hard to make good decisions until you are on the upward swing toward the new beginning. Get help to get through the fog. If you are a verbal processor, talk it through with a trusted colleague. The best decision will surface.

- Learn to live with ambiguity. This was a required management skill during the 1990s, and it's still necessary today. As Dewitt Jones says, "Learn to live with uncertainty, yet act with confidence."

Proceed/Perform

- Make the most informed and holistic decision you can make with the time and information available. Then stand by it. Commit to a time frame for the plan to be implemented. Don't shift gears so quickly that your employees lose confidence in your decision making. You want to avoid giving the impression that you are wishy-washy or floundering.

- A few months after launching the implementation, if it is not working, or if more data becomes available, allow for input and continuous improvement. Listen non-defensively to important feedback and suggestions.

Most importantly, while leading people through change, pay attention to your people! Don't get so consumed by the tasks of the change that you lose the commitment and momentum of your people. After all, they are the ones you are counting on to move the change to a successful outcome.

CHAPTER 5

EMBRACING A DIVERSE WORKFORCE

Effective leaders shape their organization's culture. Increasingly, diversity is a value that is actively fostered. Leaders can set the tone so the environment is welcoming and accepting of individuals from all races, ethnicities, religions, and genders, with a minimum of misunderstanding.

The fundamental challenge of leading a diverse workforce is helping people manage their own response to differences. When someone is different in any way—looks, opinions, beliefs, dialect, age, etc.—the first response from many people is discomfort. It's a fairly normal human response. How that discomfort is managed is what matters.

Recognizing when you're in a situation that's outside of your comfort zone marks a choice point. When you choose to take responsibility for your feelings, this choice point causes a shift. As a result, you start choosing to behave more effectively with others.

Today, the term "diversity" is more inclusive of *all* differences. In the workplace, this includes work style, learning style, communication style, goal-orientation, level of ability, productivity, part-timers, volunteers, union, non-union, and even music preferences. In addition, leaders must continue to be attentive to the areas of protected class, including age, race, color, national origin, gender/sexual orientation, FMLA/ADA accommodations, religion, etc.

Some government employees have expressed frustration with the emphasis on diversity, saying, "It's just common sense. We all treat each other respectfully here. We have to. It's policy!"

While this may be true, some people are unaware of the ways in which their behavior impacts others or the ways in which their biases towards others are revealed. Perhaps they don't want to admit their feelings about their differences with others.

Here are three examples of actual workplace situations involving diversity issues:

1. In a public health department, a new program was started to address the needs of HIV/STD clients. A few of the nurses and clerical support staff felt a personal conflict with being assigned to this program. They had faith and/or personal morality beliefs that resulted in their feeling uncomfortable. They expressed judgment and, in some cases, even disgust when working with this group of clients. When they discussed this with their supervisor, individually and as a group, they were told that their conduct was unprofessional and unacceptable. The supervisor held them to a standard of serving the customers in need, regardless of economic, health, or other conditions. He reminded them that as public servants their customer base includes a variety of protected classes. The employees were told that if they could not perform their duties as

assigned, they would be seen as non-compliant. A couple of the employees chose to leave, and the others sought transfers to other departments or agencies.

▶ How would you respond in this situation? What policies or standards would you use to support your position?

2. You manage a department that is experiencing layoffs, and you hear two employees talking with each other about the unfairness of the layoff process relative to seniority language in the union contract. One employee said, "There are other employees who are more senior to Mary Lou, but because she speaks Spanish, she gets to keep her job. That's unfair!"

▶ How would this situation be handled in your organization? Do you have layoff guidelines stating the need to retain employees who are bilingual?

3. In an HR department, one of the recruiters felt strongly about possible candidates who she saw as being "different," and wanted to screen them out. She expressed her concern in a staff meeting about candidates that she knew were gay, Muslim, or some other "type" of person that she thought would be "less desirable" in the organization. The HR manager was stunned at the comment, knowing that the employee had attended classes on preventing harassment, valuing diversity, and respect training with all the other employees.

At the same time, the manager was appreciative that the employee was willing to express her concern. The manager said that the recruiter would need to put aside her personal beliefs and screen solely on the basis of the criteria given to her by the department manager hiring for the position. She was advised to be objective in scoring the candidate's qualifications. The recruiter replied that, in all honesty, she was not sure if that would be possible. The manager thanked her for her honesty and said they would need to talk further about the issue in private and discuss possible options.

▶ How would this situation be handled in your organization? What are the policies that support non-discrimination in the hiring process (or other HR processes)?

In addition to lifestyle, ethic, or religious differences, there are also impacts that result from the fact that both private industry and government exists within a global context. Many global issues impact us at a local level—the global economy, outsourced jobs, immigration issues, English and non-English speaking clients/employees, dependency on foreign oil, etc. While these issues may not affect *your* workplace directly, people tend to have and express very strong opinions about them. How these issues are discussed among your employees can have a big impact on your workplace if the comments include bias, prejudice, or negative stereotypes.

The goal, of course, is to encourage all employees to see differences as strengths, something to be valued and appreciated. This may be easier said than done if some of your employees were raised with an attitude of negativity, prejudice, or an "enemy mentality." Your willingness to seek out, listen to, and incorporate diverse opinions will help provide a model for your employees to follow.

Two issues that are prevalent in most workplaces today are multiculturalism and the multi-generational workplace. First, let's look at a couple definitions of *multiculturalism.*

Multiculturalism is the doctrine that several different cultures (rather than one national culture) can coexist peacefully and equitably in a single country.[33]

Multiculturalism: a system of beliefs and behaviors that recognizes and respects the presence of all diverse groups in an organization or society, acknowledges and values their socio-cultural differences, and encourages and enables their continued contribution within an inclusive cultural context which empowers all within the organization or society.[34]

▶ How would *you* define multiculturalism?

Is multiculturalism possible in a government organization? Opinions vary, widely. Some say, "No, it's not!" And they feel strongly about it. Others believe that it is indeed possible, and they contend that it is essential.

Part of the challenge for most government bureaucracies is that by nature they are structured for long-term status quo. They emphasize policy and conformity, and expect compliance with regulations. How, then, is it possible to also value individuality and allow flexibility in changing times?

While these may appear to be philosophical or rhetorical questions, they are not. These issues can present as very practical daily challenges for supervisors and decision-makers. In full recognition of all the inherent paradoxes and dilemmas, it is still possible for leaders to teach their employees, peers and customers how to communicate respectfully and treat one another with courtesy and consideration.

The first step is for you as a leader to know how *you* feel about these issues, and then clearly communicate and clarify what you expect from your employees. Take time now to reflect on and answer the questions on the next page.

▶ How do you feel about leading and managing a multicultural workforce?

▶ How do you feel about serving a multicultural customer base?

▶ What are the diversity issues that you face in your workplace and service delivery?

▶ What steps are you taking to address these issues?

▶ Why should you be concerned with embracing multiculturalism?

If personal ethics and cultural norms are not compelling enough, a look at the numbers may be motivating. The 2010 census clearly indicates that the ethnically diverse populations in the U.S. are growing significantly. As a leader/manager, you want to recruit and retain the best employees. Odds are, some of the best people—those with the skills, talents and abilities you need—are not currently in your employ. They are the men and women you will be hiring next month, or next year. Building a strong team that includes people who inherently hold a variety of individual experiences, backgrounds, and cultures gives you greater strength. A diverse team can view problems and challenges through a wider variety of lenses. That creates a richer collaboration, more innovation, and better outcomes.

Another diversity issue that is impacting most workplaces across the US is that of *the generations*. Some organizations now have as many as six distinct generations working side-by-side, and the differences are significant.

Opinions vary as to where the lines are drawn between one generation and the next. The standard wisdom used to be that a generational group was identified every twenty years, but now the cycles seem to be moving faster. (Gen X and Y hovered around ten years each.) WWII and the years immediately after were the defining line for many boomers, but now we are more likely to parse out our generations over technological usage and other cultural developments.

Defining and understanding generational differences is a rich sociological conversation, and the variety of opinions contributes mightily to the complexity of the discussion. The following generation names and dates are rough guidelines, plus or minus a few years. Again, opinions vary widely.

The six generations now present in the workplace include:

- Traditionals (born 1920-1939)
- Baby Boomers (born 1940-1960)
- Tweeners (born 1960-65)
- Gen X (born 1965-82)
- Gen Y - Millenials (born 1983-2000)
- Gen Z (born 2001-2020)

While many organizations expect their employees to be cooperative team players and effective communicators, this extremely diverse range of generational differences can bring a whole new level of challenge and complexity to all manner of interpersonal behaviors.

For example, consider the generational differences in how employees approach work ethic, desire for time off, entitlement, respect for authority, rewards and recognition, loyalty, and technology. The ways in which individuals and groups of individuals do or do not place value on these characteristics can cause friction—sometimes significant friction.

People have expectations of one another, consciously and subconsciously. We can't *not* have expectations. It's inherent in who we are and how we interact with other people. Friction occurs when expectations are not clearly communicated and agreed upon, and when others don't meet our expectations.

Here's a classic example of this pattern: suppose you have a Baby Boomer, Joe. He prides himself on never having missed a day of work in twenty years. Along comes Tyler, and he's from Gen Y. Tyler uses all his sick days and vacation days as they accrue to do the things he enjoys. It's not hard to imagine that Joe may see Tyler as a slacker with a poor work ethic and a bloated sense of entitlement. Joe finds himself shaking his head and wondering, "Where is his loyalty? And what's happened to having a strong work ethic?"

Tyler, on the other hand, doesn't see what the problem is. He's earned those days, and he's entitled to them. He lives for his passions and works to fund them. He does good work. He's made so many improvements that all the systems run smarter and faster than the way they did before, so what's the problem? Tyler is offended by Joe's judgment, and Joe is offended by Tyler's work style.

► What generational concerns and beliefs are you noticing with your workforce or customers?

► What are some ways in which you are addressing these concerns?

Now, blending multiculturalism and the generations together, the new census data shows that Generation Y is the most racially and ethnically diverse generation in American history. One-third identifies with a race other than Caucasian, compared to 85 percent of those aged sixty-five and older who consider themselves to be "white."[35]

Given the inevitable continued growth of diversity in the workplace, it is incumbent upon leaders and managers to set the tone. Following are several examples:

- Set and lead the cultural norms in your group.
- Clarify behavioral expectations and demonstrate how to be considerate and inclusive.
- Teach your team how to practice non-defensive communication.
- Model being respectful in all of your interactions.

When there are breaches (as there will be), consider it a "teachable moment," and use it as an opportunity to reset expectations and reinforce the new norms.

What does "Embracing Diversity in the Workplace" have to do with Leadership and Motivation? When employees feel included, respected and safe to be who they are, morale and motivation increase significantly. When employees feel that the workplace is a hostile environment, that they feel targeted and no one really listens to them, you will also see low trust, high gossip, fear, suspicion, and anxiety. Which environment would you like to work in? Which environment do you want to foster for your employees?

When employees feel valued and honored for their individual gifts and talents, they like coming to work. Most employees come to work hopeful that it will be a good day, and want to do a good job. Acting as a catalyst, what can you do to elevate that hopeful energy into something inclusive, collaborative, motivating, and synergistic? It starts with you. Step up and take the lead.

CHAPTER 6

HOLDING PEOPLE ACCOUNTABLE

Much has been written about accountability in government. Most of it has to do with fiscal responsibility, ethics, and transparency. But that is not the total picture.

Accountability is an important aspect of leading and managing a department, project, or team. Employees remain motivated and respond well when leaders actively manage accountability, which means they hold their employees accountable, and they themselves are willing to be held accountable by their peers and superiors.

Here's an example: as a facilitator and mediator, I have worked with quite a few groups that have not been held accountable. I have seen, time and again, that groups that fail to practice accountability have a much harder time bringing issues to resolution. They also have a harder time implementing agreed upon changes, and stabilizing themselves once changes are implemented. While holding people accountable may not always be comfortable, in the final analysis, it is much more efficient than avoidance.

But that does not mean people know how to go about doing it. For example, one new supervisor asked me, "What exactly are we supposed to hold people accountable for? We're told to be accountable, but we're not taught how to hold others accountable."

I thought it was a good question, so I asked the class participants to brainstorm a list based on their experiences. What should people be held accountable for? Here's a partial list of responses:

- Policies, procedures, and performance expectations
- Follow-through on commitments made to customers and coworkers
- Timeliness, such as showing up on time, meeting deadlines, etc.
- Behavioral and interpersonal expectations
- Projects delegated to another person and quality of the work
- Tasks left undone by one employee, and the burden is transferred to others to complete

In addition to this list, what are some behaviors that employees believe *leaders* should be held accountable for? The following list contains responses from employees when asked this question:

- Consistent application and enforcement of policies
- Treating employees fairly
- Knowledge about the department processes and individual employees' job responsibilities

- Coaching and educating before starting discipline
- Follow-through on commitments
- Communicating in advance about upcoming changes
- Fair and equitable performance evaluations based on objective observations throughout the year, and free of evaluator bias
- Defending or supporting employees when there are inter-departmental or interagency conflicts
- Modeling the appropriate behavior when there is a conflict or a policy issue

▶ What else would you add to these lists?

When a manager holds staff accountable, a sense of trust develops. When there is a sense of trust, there are fewer employee relations issues, less gossip, less fault-finding, less blaming and shaming, less wasted time, and more productivity. When there is an environment of trust, employees look forward to coming to work, they get along with one another much better, take responsibility for their assigned work, are more willing to be held accountable, and they respect their director/manager more. Do you think accountability affects motivation? Yes, absolutely!

What Stops Leaders From Holding Others Accountable?

Most often, it is because they don't want to hurt anyone's feelings, or they have a tendency to be conflict avoidant.

However, they sidestep the issue at a great price. Doing nothing has some very real costs and consequences, both for leaders and those they manage, lead, and serve. Some costs and consequences are fairly easy to measure, and others are harder to quantify, but they all have a very real impact. For example: lower morale, unspoken discontent, diminished individual and team performance, dissatisfied customers, substandard work quality, a culture of blame, missed deadlines, no established measures or metrics, inconsistent policy enforcement, and indirectly rewarding irresponsible behavior. Perhaps the worst consequence of not holding others accountable is the negative perception of the leader. It creates the perception that you don't treat people fairly and equitably, and you lose the respect and loyalty of the very people you need on your team.

It takes courage to step up to the task of actively managing accountability. Once a leader realizes that they do in fact need to manage accountability, they can put a plan together to meet with the employee and get the ball rolling to improve the behavior or performance.

Five Steps to Accountability

How do you go about holding someone accountable? Here is a list of five steps:

1. **Clarify expectations.** What are the expected behaviors? What are the performance benchmarks? Does your employee have a clear and accurate understanding of what is expected?

2. **Identify the performance gap.** What is happening now? What does/does not meet expectations? What needs to change?

3. **Actively engage others in exploring options**. Accountability works best when all pertinent parties are actively involved in exploring options, including the person being held accountable. Don't just tell them what to do. Actively involve them in identifying avenues for improvement. Allow and encourage them to contribute to the process of developing solutions. Ask, "What do you think would make a difference? How can this performance gap be bridged?"

4. **Agree on action steps.** Remember, action steps need to be clear, behaviorally specific, and actionable. Clarify roles, establish timelines, and identify intended outcomes. Ask for agreement and commitment. Don't just write up a document for them to sign.

5. **Monitor progress.** Observe and provide coaching on the behaviors and performance identified and discussed. Set progress check dates (and keep them!) until the new goals or behaviors have stabilized.

▶ Before going any further, take a moment and think of an example from your workplace where you could apply these five steps of accountability.

Situation:

1. What expectations were communicated?

2. How would you identify the performance gap?

3. What options can you recommend? How will you engage the individual in a discussion about options?

4. What action steps would you like to see happen?

5. How would you monitor progress?

The Complexities of Holding Others Accountable

So far, we've just covered the basics. Now, let's get into a few of the complexities related to accountability.

One problem is that there are directors, managers, and supervisors who still are not comfortable holding others accountable. There are also those who think the policies and procedures do not apply to them. Imagine that! These problems have escalated in recent years due to the increased number of leadership transitions and the resulting increase in newly hired, promoted or appointed leaders. Most leaders are amazing and talented people. However, some of the new leaders are technically sound, but ineffective as leaders and managers.

So, what if...

a) One department's collections have gone past ninety days without any consequence to the customer or staff, and now it is affecting the larger organization's cash flow?

b) A manager has documented twelve months of coaching for an ineffective supervisor, but the issues remain, and the manager is unwilling to move it forward into a disciplinary process?

c) A department head refuses to address an escalating issue of abuse because the alleged offender is six months from retirement, and he is a fishing buddy?

d) An elected official has turned a blind eye to a harassment situation in her office, even though several different employees have complained about it over the last four months?

e) A division director is consistently over budget with no negative consequences, because another program covers their variances, and the whole matter is pretty well hidden inside the larger departmental budget?

These are just a few examples of situations in which the lack of action leads to larger system impacts, and, ultimately, significantly more cost.

How Do You Hold the Leaders Accountable?

Similarly, how do we hold elected officials accountable? In all fairness, it needs to be said that getting to the point where you feel you need to take the measures detailed below is not the norm. Rather, it is the exception to the rule. Most bureaucratic leaders and elected officials are quite willing to conduct themselves in a manner befitting a civil servant.

Given that caveat, let's address the question. Holding others accountable can be challenging enough at a peer level and with those who report up to you. Add in the power dynamic intrinsic in a hierarchy, and it gets more complicated.

How do you address accountability with those who are above you? Odds are great that you have known managers who need more managing and leaders who need to be led when it comes to accountability. It's a very common but still uncomfortable, and potentially intimidating, situation. So what do you do?

First of all, it depends on the organization's culture and the real or perceived risks of speaking up. What might happen if you shine a light on the taboo topic or that untouchable person? What are the risks of moving forward? What are the risks of doing nothing? What is this situation costing you— emotionally, physically, and psychologically? What is it costing the organization in terms of absenteeism, increased sick leave, etc.?

If the risk is low to moderate, you might start by talking one-on-one with the individual. Clearly state your request, using all the effective communication skills you have developed. If you have tried two or three times with no improvement, you might want to gather a few more leaders to have a group "intervention." If the risk is higher, you'll probably want to enlist the assistance of the HR manager or, at the very least, secure the assistance of a facilitator or mediator to help create a safe environment for dialogue and resolution.

Practically speaking, the most powerful tool for addressing accountability issues with leaders is peer pressure. In most cases, once confronted, the individual will wake up enough to the impact of their behaviors that they will be willing to make the requested changes. Think about basic behavior modification: everyone has something that rewards them for continuing their behavior.

If you can stop rewarding the undesired behavior, chances are it will stop. And you might need to change your behavior as well. For example, you might start saying positive comments when you see a desired behavior, making a corrective comment when you see an undesired behavior, staying silent if you used to laugh at inappropriate jokes, or letting the individual know you won't be covering for him or her anymore.

If he or she is still unwilling to comply, or if the changes don't stabilize, you may need more leverage. In that case, the best next step is taking the high road… go higher up the chain of command. It may require bringing the issue to the attention of the executive team, the board, the state professional association, the licensing agency, the citizen petition process, or perhaps entering into a mediation process.

What Stops People From Holding Leaders Accountable?

In general, fear, intimidation, and a discomfort with making oneself vulnerable are just a few things that stop employees from holding leaders accountable. For example:

- Fear of retribution can take the form of blatant or subtle behaviors toward the one who raises the issue. Retaliation or retribution has been demonstrated through unfair treatment of the "whistleblower," demotions, constructive discharge, giving "the silent treatment" or otherwise creating a hostile work environment. Quite often, it is done by simply creating adverse conditions that foster undue emotional distress.

- Fear of face-to-face confrontation may involve an underlying anxiety about conflict and/or an uncertainty that you will be able to "hold your center" and thus gain a satisfactory resolution in a direct interaction. When this is the case, people often resort to indirect communication, whether it is "handling it through email" or talking with a third party instead of dealing directly.

- Fear of losing your job may be more of a perceived fear if you are protected by a bargaining contract, whereas it may be a real possibility with an at-will employee.

- Fear of losing the leader, and the hassle of having to replace (and often retrain) a new leader may cause executives to tolerate otherwise unacceptable behavior longer than usual.

- Intimidation is often a factor when an employee wants to confront a person who they see as being aggressive, dismissive, threatening, or in a position of authority over them. In such cases, perception is reality. So if you believe someone is exerting "power over" you, it is real for you, whether or not it would be "real" to an outside observer.

- Anticipation of discomfort in having to work with someone post-conflict. We all carry awareness that conflicts do not always truly resolve, and this is a very real concern. However, it is also true that when people in conflict can move past the venting stage and go full course into actual resolution, greater trust and stronger working relationships can evolve. When people have a reason to expect that the conflict will go full cycle and actually get resolved satisfactorily, it is much easier to summon the courage to hold leaders accountable.

- The belief that the person is technically a good performer and you don't want to risk losing his or her skill. Some department heads are willing to tolerate poor relationship skills because the technical skills are highly specialized, or there is only one person who has those skills. In more recent years, organizations expect all employees to be competent both in technical and relational skills. Cross-training also may help this situation.

- "Wait-and-see" is a commonly held attitude. "Maybe if I just wait a little longer, things will get better…" While an outside observer can easily identify the risks of such a passive orientation, for the individual who is waiting, it makes perfect sense. This attitude indicates a protective, defensive approach. It's seen as a low-risk option.

- The belief that "it's just easier if I do it myself." If you see the leader as being less competent, you can just do it yourself and then you know it will be done "right." Since you will do it for them, it relieves them of the responsibility to get the work done themselves. In essence, you are rewarding their irresponsible behavior. This approach may be efficient in the moment, but can have problematic long-term consequences.

▶ What would you add to this list? What causes *you* to hesitate when you know you need to confront someone or hold someone accountable?

Who's Responsible for Holding Leaders Accountable?

It's clear that we all have expectations of our leaders, but what happens when it is the leader who is not meeting performance expectations? Who follows up and tracks recurring incidents?

It's nice to think that "it's everyone's job," but we've all seen that when it's "everyone's job" what often happens is that nobody actually does anything. Does this little story remind you of any experiences you've had?

> This is a story about four people: Everybody, Somebody, Anybody, and Nobody.
>
> There was an important job to be done and Everybody was asked to do it. Everybody was sure Somebody would do it. Anybody could have done it, but Nobody did it. Somebody got angry about that because it was Everybody's job. Everybody thought Anybody could do it, but Nobody realized that Everybody wouldn't do it. It ended up that Everybody blamed Somebody when Nobody did what Anybody could have done.[36]

Let's take a closer look at typical government workplace constituents and their possible roles in holding leaders accountable:

- **Employees** often are the ones who receive the unfair treatment by leaders. However, employees are most often afraid of or intimidated by management. Some managers who are less willing to take corrective feedback from an employee have been known to say, "If I want your input, I'll ask for it." To those who use this comment, I would like to refer them to the section on Non-Defensive Communication.

  It is important to recognize that there is a difference between feedback and insubordination. With feedback, there is a concern or a willingness to suggest an area of improvement. Effective leaders are willing to hear this information and respond appropriately.

  Insubordination, on the other hand, is seen as defiance on the part of the employee—not following direction, an unwillingness to comply, and a repeated questioning or argumentative pattern with the leader. These behaviors can come across as "acting out" because the employee disagrees or didn't get his or her way, but they also tend to undermine the leader's authority. Insubordination is not usually seen as a constructive approach to resolving a conflict; but sometimes, it can bring the issue to the attention of the union and the next level of management. Perhaps a more effective approach for the employee would be to bring the issue to higher management after an unsuccessful attempt to resolve the issue with the direct supervisor, and without engaging in the defiant behaviors at all.

- **Union Stewards** are responsible for intervening on behalf of the employees when an inequity of power is seen, or when they need to help interpret the contract language that applies to a conflict situation. The Union Steward can help bring light to the situation between the employee and the leader, or bring the situation to the attention of upper management or HR to help resolve the issue. In these cases, there is a better chance that a written agreement will provide documentation that can be used in a follow-up meeting in the event that no behavior change has occurred.

- **Human Resources** can provide guidance related to policy and union contracts, but in most organizations they have no authority over department management. The role of the HR manager or analyst is one of advice, guidance and, sometimes, enforcement. Often, the HR professionals are approached by department employees with an expectation that "HR will fix it for us." That approach usually comes from the place of powerlessness or hopelessness; the belief that there's nothing we can do, or that nothing will ever change. In truth, HR can provide options and legal parameters. The decision-making accountability rests with that manager or department head, not HR.

  When major issues arise, the HR professionals will most often be part of a disciplinary team, along with legal counsel, risk management, the chief administrative officer, the agency director, and others deemed necessary. The HR manager may also act as a facilitator between department management, or between departments, to help prevent the need for further mediation or arbitration. HR can also be active in tracking and monitoring incidents, especially recurring incidents in any one department or patterns across the organization.

- **Department Heads (Directors)** ultimately are responsible for the conduct of their managers and supervisors. However, in many cases, the department heads are unaware of the issues. In situations where they are aware, the recommended approach is to enter into a process similar to progressive discipline. The department head documents conversations with the leader and monitors the behavior over time to ensure improvement. With an at-will employee, a department head is not required to use due process, and has the authority to suspend, demote, or terminate someone who is classified as at-will. However, it is strongly recommended by HR and legal professionals that a department head provide the proper documentation prior to taking adverse employment actions with anyone, especially at-will employees.

  When an employee brings a concern to you about their supervisor, be sure to keep that person informed of the complaint status. Follow up to let the employee know you took action to improve the situation. More often than not, employee discontent comes from the perception that nothing was done, when in actuality, it's usually poor communication on the part of management, not following up to provide closure.

- **Peers** at the supervisory, management or executive levels can have a profound impact on the conduct of leaders. If the leadership team has documented standards of conduct and leadership competencies, those written standards can be brought "to the table" when discussing your concerns with a peer leader.

  While some may still have an attitude that "You're not my boss. Why should I listen to you?" many leadership teams have evolved to a point of valuing input from peers. Having written standards (forms) aids in depersonalizing sensitive issues, and provides a mechanism for engaging discussions. When peers raise their concerns and maintain a clearly positive intent, it is likely to result in behavior change sooner than later.

  Some elected officials may take the position that their peers have no authority over them, since the citizens elected them. In this case, first of all, it is important to remember that their peers and employees are also citizens. Secondly, the peers should prepare some next-step options, if the elected official is not a willing participant. A few suggestions are presented below under "If the issue remains, what else can you do?"

- **The Legal Department**, available within most government organizations, has legal staff with employment law expertise that can intervene to help employees and management with issues of compliance and policy violation. Legal counsel can help interpret policies, clarify priorities between federal mandates and protected classes, and ensure consistent language used within the policies, personnel rules, and bargaining contracts.

- **Citizens** are usually not aware of internal management conduct. However, sometimes citizens are members of a committee or become aware of misconduct through a newspaper article. In either case, when citizens become aware of a problem, whether leadership or organizational misconduct, they have daily access to public officials through phone calls, letters, emails, public forums, budget hearings, newspaper editorials, and now Facebook, Twitter, and blogging.

For more extreme measures, citizens can take action through a petition process to recall the elected official. If there are enough signatures on the petition, the recall process may result in the elected official submitting his or her resignation. If not, a special election may be initiated, the results of which could cause the official's removal.

The recall process varies between states regarding the minimum number of signatures and the time limit to qualify, as well as the handling of recalls once they qualify. "In some states, a recall triggers a simultaneous special election, where the vote on the recall, as well as the vote on the replacement if the recall succeeds, are on the same ballot….In other states, a separate special election is held after the target is recalled, or a replacement is appointed by the Governor or some other state authority."[37]

This raises the question: *How does someone qualify to become an elected official?* Most often, the information in the election pamphlet is submitted by the candidates themselves. While there is usually a review process with the appropriate political committee, the candidate's qualifications are presented in brief (and are often quite vague), and rarely are the job competencies stated that would give voters clarity about what the position entails. Even when an elected official gets into office, often the job description is vague. In fact, rarely are management competencies identified for state and local elected leadership positions. For many voters, this process does not inspire confidence in the candidate, let alone the system.

In Chapter 1, we discussed the difference between leadership and management. Now, let's briefly look at the role of an elected official as a department head and leader.

Many offices of elected officials have fewer than twenty people. In most of these cases, the elected official is the department head, supervisor, and operations manager. If this person is a good politician, but a weak leader, who will the employees go to for answers and decisions? If this person is not a competent manager, the impact on the employees can be significant, and sometimes with devastating consequences. Other department heads who are "at-will" employees can be suspended or terminated if they are not meeting performance goals and standards.

How can employees trust and respect their elected department head, when they see him or her behaving as if the policies do not apply to them? How can employees deeply commit to goals when they feel they are given lip-service and big picture philosophy rather than clear direction and practical strategies? How can citizens build trust in government leaders if the leaders behave one way in a public forum, and another way when they are with employees in the office? (Yes, the employees get paid to work, but they are also citizens.)

Most of us are aware that our election process needs improvement. The process of qualifying elected officials is one area that needs significant revision if government leaders are to meet the needs of their employees and the citizens they serve.

Clearly, "everybody" has a role in holding leaders accountable. But what if "nobody" does anything? It takes courage and conviction to bring light to situations in which people in authority are called to task. In the event that an issue escapes the satisfactory action of all of the people listed above, there are still other options to help resolve the matter.

If the issue remains unresolved, what else can you do?

Many local services and organizations provide resources for more difficult situations. Here are a few options:

- **Bureau of Labor and Industries (BOLI) and the Equal Employment Opportunities Commission (EEOC).** These organizations can help to investigate a situation or an entire organization where there are concerns related to harassment, discrimination, wage and hour disputes, and non-compliance with other state and federal laws.

- **Ethics Commission**. If there is an ethics violation related to elections practices, spending of government funds, harassment and other state specified codes of conduct, the Ethics Commission will investigate and provide assistance in resolving these situations.

- **State and federal associations**. Most government offices and agencies are linked to professional organizations, for example, the state or national association for sheriffs, assessors, health professionals, district attorneys, tax collectors, etc. More often than not, the state or federal office will take action to hold a local official accountable when alleged to be out of compliance with their code of conduct and professional ethics. The end result of this action may also lead to the tarnishing of someone's credibility and reputation with professional associates. This potential threat is often the motivator for the official to change his or her behavior or resign from the position to prevent this from happening.

- **Local newspaper**. If all else fails, you can always write to your local newspaper and submit an editorial with your complaint. Elected officials do not want bad press, if they're at all interested in being re-elected. So this is often a viable option. You have to be willing to have your name printed with the article, however, as most newspapers do not allow anonymous editorials.

- **Legal Representation**. By far, this will be your most expensive option, but it may be the best way to move something forward. Sometimes, it takes someone who knows how to navigate the legal system to help you get your message across to the right people.

As stated earlier, most of these options are extreme and will only need to be used in rare instances. In my experience, most government leaders are dedicated to serving their communities, customers, and employees.

My main point in sharing this information is to take a good hard look at levels of accountability and to briefly explore some areas in need of improvement.

As you reflect upon the information that was just covered, think about how you would respond in a situation where someone needed to be held accountable. What are you really willing to do?

▶ What are you willing to do to hold another person accountable?

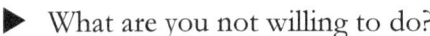

▶ What are you not willing to do?

▶ What are you willing to live with if you decide not to take action?

We've been looking deep into current issues related to accountability in government. It's like really seeing the elephant in the room. In his book, *Driving Fear Out of the Workplace*, Dan Oestreich talks about creating a safe forum to address the "taboos, undiscussables and untouchables."[38] Indeed, we need more of this in government organizations, and probably in most other organizations, too.

What does this have to do with leadership and motivation? If you have ever worked in an organization where people are actually held accountable in a healthy, productive, and energizing way, then you would know how to answer this in a second. "Everything!"

Accountability starts with you. Accountability is not just about the rules and performance outcomes. It is about creating an environment of trust, consistency, fairness, equity, and, to some extent, predictability. When leaders demonstrate an ethic of accountability, people know what to expect when they do or don't do something.

When leaders are willing to listen and receive feedback non-defensively, most often their peers and employees will respond the same way, too. When there is a problem, and the leader responds to it, either by helping to resolve a work process issue, or to help correct an employee's behavior, do you think that helps motivate employees? You bet it does!

The next time you have a question about whether or not it matters that you hold someone accountable (including yourself), know this: It matters!

Effective leaders are accountable, willing to be held accountable, and willing to hold others accountable. In this way, they effectively model the behaviors that they want others to emulate. Effective leaders are courageous. They step up to accountability.

"Honesty, integrity and accountability, the values which should be the hallmark of this government…"
–Louise Slaughter, U.S., Representative (D-NY 25th District)

"Do you have the necessary courage to exhibit personal accountability? As seen through the eyes of coworkers and employees, leadership accountability is demonstrated by:

1. *Accepting complete responsibility for your behavior*

2. *Meeting/exceeding agreed upon expectations.*

3. *Admitting mistakes.*

4. *Admitting limitations of knowledge."*
–Byrd Baggett

CHAPTER 7

PERFORMANCE EVALUATION— ENGAGE!

Closely linked with the challenges of accountability are the ways in which performance is evaluated. The performance review process has been evolving over the last twenty years to be more participative, frequent, and inclusive of customer and peer feedback. One of the challenges is the lack of consistency in the way performance reviews are conducted across all employees, and across an entire organization. Government is no exception.

> "70 *percent of employees* are *dissatisfied* with the performance appraisal process in their companies. Likewise, according to the *Society for Human Resources Management, 90 percent of human resources managers are dissatisfied* with the performance appraisal systems used by their companies."[39]

Clearly, based on this research, a significant portion of employees feel that performance evaluations are meaningless, unfair, and anxiety-producing (if not painful). Other surveys indicate that among government employee responders, 85 percent felt the same. That is a shocking statistic! It indicates a significant problem in the way that performance evaluations are conducted.

The good news is, as leaders, you can do something about it! If you are truly serious about improving employee motivation and morale, then you can begin to change the statistics by creating a performance review process that is oriented toward growth and development. To take on such a challenge, start with a focus on coaching. Then you would continue by creating a process wherein the employee is an active participant and partner in setting goals, along with outcomes and timelines. Your process would need to include the provisions for documenting results, engaging each participant in a self-evaluation, and then collecting customer feedback from those who are internal or external to the organization.

Anecdotal evidence indicates that changing to this sort of "no surprises" evaluation process will shift the culture within just one or two years. Time and again, I have seen the resulting increases in proactive ownership, personal responsibility and increased accountability. This participative approach does not require any large bureaucratic decree. It can be done by you in your department or on your team, without any major revision in the official form of the evaluation process. It is simply a revision in *your* style.

Let's look at an example. A few years ago, I was called in to consult on a fairly classic situation. There was an employee who was not performing well in a certain skill area, and he received fairly low ratings on his performance evaluation form. After meeting with the union steward for advice, he complained to his department head. His complaint: he was not aware of the performance expectation, received no coaching, and there was no progress check prior to the evaluation. The reality: this was, in fact, the truth. Now, I'm going to risk saying something potentially provocative: *What is the responsibility of the supervisor when his or her employees are not performing well? And what are the consequences for the supervisor? Who administers those consequences?*

When an employee is not performing, the supervisor may need coaching or a corrective action plan as much as the employee. My best guess is that in as many as 50 percent of discipline cases, there should be a plan for both the employee and the supervisor. What a difference this would make in creating a culture of accountability!

Good leaders take accountability for the performance of their department and their employees. Good leaders, managers and supervisors are clear about what they expect. They monitor performance all year long to ensure that the individual and departmental goals are met.

One more soapbox discussion about performance evaluations. Feedback to management is critical, and often it is completely absent. Most government organizations do not have a 360-degree feedback process. (If your organization does, I applaud you!) When you consider that most other public and private organizations have been doing 360-degree reviews for decades, it makes me wonder, as a taxpayer, how effective our elected and bureaucratic leaders are. If they are not receiving feedback from employees and are not held fully accountable in the evaluation process, how *can* they be effective in their leadership role?

I often wonder what leaders are afraid of when they fail to support a 360-degree feedback process. The feedback is intended to be supporting, coaching and developmental, not punitive. Traditionally, government leadership has been granted tremendous levels of trust, and only held accountable for the end results. Perhaps it is time to look more closely at how well they are behaving and performing, and how they are achieving those results. The bottom line: *low accountability breeds low performance.*

One manager actually said to me, *"Management doesn't need to be evaluated. We're exempt."* My jaw dropped! Where in the definition of "exempt employees" does it mention that performance reviews are not applicable? It then occurred to me that this attitude may be at the core of the separation between management and staff—the sense of us-and-them that the unions work so hard to bridge. If even some of our management folks believe that performance reviews do not apply to them, this attitude engenders a culture of entitlement and inequity. It is hard to over-estimate the corrosive effects of this assumption of privilege.

Similarly, just because someone was elected to an office does not mean that his or her employees want to go where they are being led. If the employees feel hopeless to do anything to improve their leader's behavior, because of the perception that elected officials are "untouchable," the employee may reach a point of readiness to call an attorney. Doesn't it make more sense to just spend some time listening to the feedback of your employee-citizens?

Leaders must be willing, capable and courageous enough to receive feedback non-defensively from their employees (i.e., their internal customers), as well as from their community partners, the citizens they serve. We have already touched on non-defensive communication and addressed how important it is to receive feedback as well as to give it.

When employees are not allowed to give feedback, this barrier fosters a culture of learned helplessness, hopelessness, stagnation, and suppression. (Please notice that these traits are not necessarily inherent in any individual employee. They are learned from and reinforced by the environment.) More often than not, you as a leader are less effective when your employees are cut off from being able to give you feedback. Conversely, when employees *are* invited to give feedback—safely and without retribution—they feel more empowered to make positive changes, and that benefits the entire system, including you.

Finally, there is a practice that I have taught for years in performance management classes:

Separate progressive discipline and performance evaluations!

When leaders meet with their employees, it is critical to differentiate between a progressive discipline meeting and a performance evaluation meeting. These are two separate conversations and two separate documents. To foster a trusting relationship with employees, it is important to provide coaching *all year long*. In this way, you can stay on top of an employee's progress or lack thereof.

If you have documented a gap in expected vs. actual performance, it is incumbent upon you as a manager/leader to talk with the person *immediately*. Schedule this meeting well in advance of any evaluation meeting, to give the employee an opportunity to change his or her behavior before the evaluation is finalized. Involve the employee in determining realistic options and solutions to the situation. This lets the employee know that you have positive intent and that you are not just waiting to "get them." Also, be clear about what is not negotiable, namely, that the performance must improve within a specified period of time.

Performance evaluations should be a summary of the activities that have occurred all year long, not a dreaded once-a-year meeting. If you have been communicating well all year, there won't be any surprises, and you can move forward by setting clear expectations for the upcoming year.

▶   As you read through this material about performance evaluations, what were your thoughts? What do you agree with? What do you disagree with?

▶ **Self-Assessment:** On a scale of 1-10 [with 1 being rarely and 10 being almost always], rate yourself on the questions below:

Question	Rating
1. Do you enjoy the annual performance evaluation process?	1 2 3 4 5 6 7 8 9 10
2. Do you meet with each employee to review his or her performance more than once a year?	1 2 3 4 5 6 7 8 9 10
3. Do you enjoy meeting with your employees for the annual review meeting?	1 2 3 4 5 6 7 8 9 10
4. Do your employees seem to enjoy the annual performance evaluation process?	1 2 3 4 5 6 7 8 9 10
5. Do you believe your employees find the performance indicators meaningful to their actual work?	1 2 3 4 5 6 7 8 9 10
6. Do you ask your employees for feedback on your performance as a supervisor?	1 2 3 4 5 6 7 8 9 10
7. If you answered "yes" to #6, do you DO anything with that information?	1 2 3 4 5 6 7 8 9 10

How did you do? If you are enjoying the process and your employees are finding meaning in their performance measures, that's a good sign!

If you are not enjoying the process year-round, as well as the annual review meeting, *what would you like to see happen differently?*

Clearly, there is a link between performance and motivation. And whether you realize it or not, there is a clear link between the way you manage performance year-round and your employees' motivation.

If employees are engaged in managing their own performance all year long, and are receiving coaching and encouragement from the leaders, they are more likely to achieve their goals and bring projects to fruition. When employees experience the accomplishment of goals and projects, they feel an increase in self-worth and confidence. When employees are recognized and praised for their accomplishments, they feel a sense of gratification and fulfillment in their work. They feel that what they are doing makes a difference. Does this affect motivation? Absolutely!

Your role as a leader is to help your employees succeed. Take the lead in helping them to set clear goals, and then monitor their progress throughout the year and provide any necessary guidance and coaching. By keeping in touch on a regular basis, you will be more aware of their progress and any stumbling blocks, and you will be better able to gauge their level of initiative, commitment and perseverance. These are the kinds of leadership behaviors that inspire motivation in an employee.

"The best way to inspire people to superior performance is to convince them by everything you do, and by your attitude, that you are wholeheartedly supporting them.
–HAROLD S. GENEEN

CHAPTER 8

STRATEGIC INNOVATION

To keep employees motivated, it is critical to maintain an innovative environment. In the past, government has seen its role as maintaining the status quo. Those days are over. There have been many instances where local and regional government agencies have been recognized for their innovative programs and new alternatives to addressing the needs of the communities. If the truth be known, these programs are all too few and far between, and are not well funded for the long-term.

Innovation in government is a paradox. On the one hand, there are almost unlimited funds for research and development. Government agencies, including the military, hire the brightest minds in the country to create new solutions and help us to see new alternative futures. These endeavors also involve highly classified, high risk, and competitive projects.

On the other hand, in local government organizations, innovation seems to be risky business. Many leaders are personally threatened by employees who think creatively and who want to move projects faster than the bureaucratic processes will allow. These employees often get frustrated and leave for a higher paying and more rewarding job in the private sector.

In one situation, a manager said to me, *"I don't want my employees to be creative. I don't want to set new goals for the next year. I just want employees who will do the same thing from one year to the next."* My reaction to this statement was fourfold: a) Yes, there is a place for those employees; b) I wouldn't want to work for you; c) You really don't want the job you have; d) That attitude is scary!

What I actually said to the manager was, *"How much turnover do you have?"* The manager replied, *"I'm constantly recruiting."* To which I asked, *"Do you think there might be a correlation?"* The manager replied, *"It never occurred to me…"* Somehow, I was not surprised.

In another situation, a conversation about management structure versus flexibility, a group of managers discussed how to enforce policies consistently, while allowing for extenuating circumstances. Here is an interesting exchange I had with a manager from that session. We'll call him Fred.

> Fred: *"Hey, they came to work for us. They read the job description. They are the ones that need to change, not us!"*

> Mary: I'm sure my facial expression said it all. After a long breath, I asked, *"Who was responsible for the hiring decision?"*

> Fred: *"I was."*

Mary: *"How much about the organizational culture is listed in your job descriptions?"*

Fred: *"Nothing."*

Mary: *"Then how does the employee learn about the culture and the policies?"*

Fred: *"The supervisor for the new employee does all that."*

Mary: *"And who is responsible for training the supervisors?"*

Fred: *"Well, they all know more about the operation, so they kind of train each other."*

Mary: *"Where it says 'creativity and flexibility' on the performance evaluation form, what exactly are you looking for there, and how do you reward that kind of behavior?"*

Fred: *"Well, I use that mainly for when they are resistant to change, not cooperating with coworkers, or demonstrating insubordinate behaviors. I figure they aren't very flexible."*

Mary: *"And how does your boss rate you on creativity and flexibility?"*

Fred shrugged but did not respond.

This was a classic example of a leader who was not only unaware of his own ineffectiveness, but also unaware of his inability to be accountable for his own actions, and those of his employees.

This innovation paradox begs the question: How do we maintain a bureaucratic structure while allowing the necessary innovation to grow with the times, and to remain competitive with private industry and the global economy?

Many government executive teams spend time doing strategic planning, whether it is annually or once every five years. Strategic planning can be very useful in providing a reality check for what's happening in the environment, and how priorities might be revised. What I hear frequently from leaders and employees is that it was a waste of time; that they talked about the same thing the last time, and that they made a nice plan that was never implemented.

One consultant friend said, "Doing strategic planning in government is like spending three days putting a plan together that was not much different than the one they created five years ago. The barriers to creative thought and risk taking were impenetrable, scary and invisible."

What will it take for some government leaders to realize that strategic planning isn't an either/or proposition—bureaucracy or creativity, but it must be both? Government organizations must introduce a willingness to innovate if they want to keep up with the pace of change and be able to retain talented employees.

Strategic Innovation

The following excerpts were written for business leaders in the for-profit sector. This model is a unique blend of strategic visioning and planning for innovation. As you read the excerpts, think about how these concepts might apply in a government organization.

"Strategic Innovation is the creation of growth strategies, new product categories, services, or business models that change the game and generate significant new value for consumers, customers and the corporation."[40]

"Strategic Innovation calls for a holistic approach that operates on multiple levels. First, it blends non-traditional and traditional approaches to business strategy, deploying the practices of Industry Foresight, Consumer/Customer Insight, and Strategic Alignment as a foundation, and supplementing them with more conventional approaches and models. Second, it combines two seemingly *paradoxical mindsets*: expansive, visionary thinking that imaginatively explores long-term possibilities; and pragmatic, down-to-earth implementation activities that lead to short-term, measurable business impact."[41]

First, let's look at some principles of innovative learning:[42]

- Anticipation—being active and imaginative rather than passive and habitual
- Learning by listening to others—valuing shared knowledge rather than dismissing others' ideas
- Participation—shaping events, rather than being shaped by them

Next, it's important to have a framework. Soren Kaplan and Derrick Palmer of Innovation Point Consulting have put forth a Strategic Innovation framework that weaves together seven dimensions to produce a portfolio of outcomes that drive organizational health: [43]

- A Managed Innovation Process—combining traditional and non-traditional approaches to business strategy. (More details later in this chapter.)
- Strategic Alignment—building support - vertical, horizontal and procedural
- Industry Foresight—understanding emerging trends
- Consumer/Customer Insight—understanding articulated and unarticulated needs
- Core Technologies and Competencies—leveraging and extending corporate assets
- Organizational Readiness—the ability to take action
- Disciplined Implementation—managing the path from inspiration to business impact

► How would you rate your organization's current level of Strategic Innovation? How would you rate your department's current level of Strategic Innovation? Consider the extent to which these principles and dimensions are (or are not) happening in your organization and your department. [5=widely encouraged and used, 1=not on the radar]

Principles	Department	Organization
Anticipation		
Learning by Listening		
Participation		
Dimensions		
A Managed Innovation Process		
Strategic Alignment		
Industry Foresight		
Consumer/Customer Insight		
Core Technologies and Competencies		
Organizational Readiness		
Disciplined Implementation		

► Are you satisfied with these results? If not, what would you like to see happen differently?

Traditional Approaches vs. Strategic Innovation

Some government leaders are deeply entrenched in public administration theories and truly don't know how to change. Other leaders came to government from private industry, and they've learned the public administration processes and adjusted to them; still others have not adjusted but seem to fight them at every turn, wanting to make improvements and increase efficiencies. If you are one of those who would like to make changes, but are not sure what or how exactly to change, the chart below might be useful.

Here is a summary of the differences between traditional approaches to strategy and Strategic Innovation:[44] [*emphasis mine**]

*A Typical Traditional Approach	The Strategic Innovation Approach
Adopts a "present to future" orientation using today as the starting point	"Starts with the end in mind" by identifying long-term opportunities and then bridges back to the present
Assumes a rule-maker/taker (defensive/follower) posture	Assumes a rule-breaker (revolutionary) posture
Accepts established business boundaries/product categories	Seeks to create new competitive space/playing fields
Focuses on incremental innovation	Seeks breakthrough, disruptive innovation while continuing to build the core
Follows traditional, linear business planning models	Marries process discipline with creative inspiration
Seeks input from obvious, traditional sources	Seeks inspiration from unconventional sources
Seeks articulated consumer needs	Seeks unarticulated consumer needs
Is technology-driven (seeks consumer satisfaction)	Is consumer-inspired (seeks consumer delight)
May have a "one-size-fits-all" organizational model	May experiment with entrepreneurial "new venture" or other organizational structures

▶ Take another look at the preceding table. Put an "X" next to the statements that describe your department right now, and circle the statements that describe your department of tomorrow.

▶ What are some steps you will take to bridge the gap? By when?

Considering the statements you selected that describe your "department of tomorrow," write at least three steps to move toward strategic innovation.

Steps:	By when:
1.	
2.	
3.	

▶ Are you willing to be accountable for taking those actions? If so, to whom will you be accountable?

One of the key factors for achieving goals is the successful implementation of your plan. How many times have you been through a survey process where you never got the results of the survey? If you did get the results, were you aware that anything was expected to change or improve? If something was changed, did you see any follow-up assessment to know what difference it made? Also, how many times have you been aware that your organization paid someone (usually an outside consultant) $50,000 or more to conduct those surveys? In general, employees' overall attitude about surveys is, *"What a waste of time and money!"*

General guideline: If you're going to do an assessment or survey, share the results with those who took the time to provide their input. Then let management, employees, and customers know about the changes, progress and outcomes you're considering, based on the responses. Otherwise, stop wasting taxpayer dollars.

When you get the results of a survey or assessment, what are the next steps to ensure a successful implementation? Here are several ideas:

- Review the report for areas of strength
- Review the report for areas that need development or improvement
- Develop an action plan to celebrate and optimize the strengths
- Develop an action plan to address and strengthen areas in need of development
- Communicate the plan and foster commitment
- Implement the plan
- Establish progress-check dates and monitor progress
- Do a follow-up assessment annually for three years and report your progress to superiors, employees and customers.

One other key point that's related to successful implementation is that plans very often fall away due to election or hiring of a new leader, when the ownership of the plan belonged to the previous leader. To sustain a successful implementation, a "transition measure" is necessary. This requires an intentional transfer of ownership to the new leader, with a commitment from the new leader to carry the process through to fruition.

Also, if you have training and organization development people on your payroll, why are you paying outside consultants to do what these folks are trained to do? They have been trained to be neutral observers, interviewers and data gatherers. Their objectives should be to analyze and summarize data, to provide recommended action plans (communications, change management and implementation), and to lead an implementation plan through to fruition.

Another general guideline: Value your internal expertise! During lean times, many employees are eager to share their solutions with managers and supervisors who are unwilling to listen. Put your egos aside and listen to your peers and employees. Admit that you have challenges, and ask for help.

Create a suggestion box process—digital or paper—where employees can give suggestions and ideas anonymously and safely. Then respond to the ideas.

There are lots of great ideas and suggestions out there, and you never know who might be carrying a viable solution. It may be someone from another department, a custodian or a mail courier. Stop paying external contractors to do what your own genius employees can contribute, given the chance. Be willing to listen. If you all reach a point where the answer is, "I don't know what else to do," then bring in someone from the outside to give you a new perspective.

Here's one more useful excerpt from Innovation Point:[45]

> "A Managed Innovation Process lies at the creative core of the approach. By facilitating the interplay between external perspectives and an organization's internal capabilities/practices—and by looking beyond the obvious—it is possible to inspire the organization's imagination to explore a diverse array of new possibilities.
>
> Strategic Innovation is not an end-state. Rather, it is a journey of open-minded exploration, experimentation, thinking, decision-making, action, results and learning, with the cycle then repeating. While there are numerous ways to effectively measure the business impact resulting from a Strategic Innovation initiative, an organization's ability to successfully innovate is less tangible, measured in terms of progress over time rather than in absolutes.
>
> The journey of Strategic Innovation calls for learning by doing—if an organization approaches a business issue and adopts the framework as its set of guiding principles, the business impact will be evident and there will be an opportunity to incorporate the learning as the first step toward building a foundation for sustainable innovation."

▶ What are some ways in which you are inviting and rewarding innovation in your workplace?

▶ What are some of the roadblocks to innovation in your office or organization?

▶ What are some ways you can remove the roadblocks to move forward?

One final provocative thought regarding innovation in government: The purpose of government is *not* sustainability of the government. The purpose of government is to serve the needs of the community.

More than ever in our country's history, this perspective seems clear. More than ever before, we need leaders who can create new inroads to service delivery rather than focus on sustaining their own position and privilege. We need courageous leaders who seek and invite creative thought, rather than those who feel insecure in the face of innovation.

It is time to put egos aside and focus on the needs of the community as a whole, not just from the perspective of one department. If the purpose of government is to serve the needs of the community, how innovatively are you doing that?

Some people may think the concepts of strategic innovation are inappropriate to government, but at this point in time, they are *critical*.

It's time to blend structure *and* creativity.

"I have pledged myself and my colleagues in the cabinet to a continuous encouragement of initiative, responsibility and energy in serving the public interest. Let every public servant know, whether his post is high or low, that a man's rank and reputation in this Administration will be determined by the size of the job he does, and not by the size of his staff, his office or his budget. Let it be clear that this Administration recognizes the value of dissent and daring – that we greet healthy controversy as the hallmark of healthy change. Let the public service be a proud and lively career..."

–Excerpt from President John F. Kennedy's
State of the Union Message. January 30, 1961

CHAPTER 9

MORE MOTIVATIONAL TIPS AND TOOLS

In preceding chapters, we have identified several areas that impact or influence employee motivation: recognition, communication, change, diversity, accountability, performance evaluations, and innovation.

Here are a several more ideas on how to motivate your employees in lean times.

DO:

- Be inspiring! Keep your own attitude up and model courageous leadership.
- Give people feedback, and thank them for doing their job. Living in lean times can be stressful. When there's extra stress in the workplace, at home, or both, just doing your regular job can be a lot to handle, and a little acknowledgment helps.
- Tell your employees what is changing, what it will look like after the change, and what their role will be—*as much in advance as possible.*
- Let people know what is *not* changing, so they can know where they might find a solid foundation on which to rest.
- Communicate *more* frequently. During change, managers often make the mistake of assuming people are so maxed out that the last thing they need is another meeting. While this *might* be true, more often it's the case that employees need the support and validation of an effective meeting to ensure that they are on track.
- If you are laying people off, take the time to assure surviving employees that they do and will have a job—if that is, indeed, the truth.
- Remember, motivation goes down when a person's energy is split. So if you have people who are thinking about leaving, or if your employees are fearful and wondering if they will be next, pay attention and provide as much encouragement as is honestly possible.
- Ask for support and re-commitment. Discuss what has changed over the years, and realize that simultaneous multiple changes with little or no down time can drive people to, and over, the edge. When those changes are longer lasting, everyone needs to develop the skill of "dealing with ambiguity." In uncertain times, resiliency is critical.
- Keep tabs on employees and how they are responding or reacting. Learn how to intervene effectively if you notice withdrawal, anger, confusion, etc.

- Develop a transition plan that covers today through to the desired end, and then monitor the implementation. Don't assume things will magically happen between now and the final state. Don't tell people, "Well, let's just wait and see…" or "We'll deal with that later." These statements indicate a lack of ability or willingness on your part to actually manage the change. As the old saying goes, "Plan your work and work your plan."

- Expect the unexpected and remain flexible. Even the most meticulous of planners cannot anticipate the unknown. The best approach is to take a deep breath and ask yourself, "How can I best respond to this?"

DON'T:

- In case I haven't said this clearly enough throughout this book, I want to say it here: Never yell at your employees! And never allow others to yell in your work environment. If you have a non-violence policy, yelling should be covered under "verbal abuse" and should no longer be tolerated. Yelling is not an effective means of motivating your employees, unless your intent is to motivate through threat and intimidation. These behaviors do not enhance a productive work environment.

- If you believe that "showing people the door" is an effective motivator, think again. Telling people "If you don't like it, leave. There are 100 other people waiting for your job" is another way to demean and demoralize your employees. The sad thing is that this attitude is common in many organizations during lean times. Some employers take advantage of their employees by overworking them and abusing them, because the employees feel they "have to stay" due to the economy. This attitude on the part of management only creates an environment of fear, and lowers trust in your ability to listen and resolve issues. Please examine your intent and find other more constructive means of relating to your employees.

Inspiration to Move Forward

We've covered a variety of topics about leadership and motivation up to this point. To move forward, consider your role as a leader and the ways you motivate and inspire others. When possible:

- Keep yourself and others motivated
- Create an environment of positive recognition and celebration
- Infuse your group with non-defensive communication skills
- Lead through times of change
- Set the parameters for embracing diversity
- Hold yourself and others accountable
- Manage and evaluate performance
- Engage strategic innovation
- Expand your resources and use motivational tools

Here are a few key points to remember from Chapters 3 to 9:

- Walk through the doors of your office inspired every day, so you can inspire others.
- Know your people well enough to know what matters to them and what motivates them.
- Find a way to balance the policy expectation of "treating all people the same" with the need to provide individualized coaching and motivation.
- Pay attention to your employees.
- Make motivation a priority of your job.
- Value your internal expertise.

▶ Before continuing to the next chapter, pause and reflect for a moment. Write down one motivational idea that you want to implement immediately.

For "Even More Motivational Ideas," see the Resources page on my website: www.marytmeyer.com

CHAPTER 10

HOW TO BUILD RESILIENCY IN LEAN AND CHALLENGING TIMES

Key topics covered in this chapter:

- What is Resiliency?
- How Resilient Are You?
- How to Keep Yourself Motivated and Resilient
- Ideas for Sustaining the Momentum
- Resiliency Summary

This book would not be complete without giving some attention to the topic of resiliency. After all, resiliency is what gives us the ability to sustain momentum during lean times.

Resiliency is learnable. There are tools you can use to build skills, and when those skills are consistently applied over time, resiliency becomes a habit.

During challenging times and constant change, resiliency is an invaluable quality in a leader and a team.

What is Resiliency?

Al Siebert, Director of The Resiliency Center, offers a couple of useful definitions:[46]

> "The ability to bounce back after being blown off course unexpectedly by the winds of change; the ability to recover quickly from setbacks.
>
> A person's ability to absorb high levels of disruptive change, bounce back, and even excel in times of change and uncertainty (while displaying minimal dysfunctional behavior)."

As a leader, what do you do personally when everything is in flux or you're feeling drained? Remember, there are plenty of things you can do to build resiliency.

First, think about the things you LOVE to do. *What fills you up?*

Take a moment to read through this list and think about how many of these things you enjoy. *Then think about the last time you actually did them!*

- Take breaks
- Breathe deeply
- Stretch
- Laugh
- Take walks
- Try yoga, qigong, or tai chi
- Take a vacation
- Go swimming
- Join a diverse group to discuss creative and synergetic ideas
- Spend time with optimistic people
- Play music
- Go to the mountain top to get some perspective!
- Play games with fun people
- Listen to children's laughter
- Get a massage, manicure or pedicure (or all three!)
- Reflect on your successes
- Find beautiful places
- Enjoy a good book or movie
- Sing your favorite song
- Get physical—play sports, go for a run, hit the gym, join a team

If you have difficulty identifying what you love to do, pay attention—that is an important awareness. Take some time to reflect. Talk with friends, colleagues and loved ones. Explore your options, try something new. Sometimes we need to discover what we truly enjoy. You may reignite a passion for a long lost pastime, or perhaps you'll discover a wonderful new hobby. Whatever the case, it's well worth the effort. Building resiliency is based on engaged authenticity and self-care. Know who you are and fill your life with what you genuinely love.[47]

How Resilient Are You?

Rate yourself from 1-5 [1 = very little, 5 = very strong] on the following statements:

____ Adapt quickly. Good at bouncing back from difficulties.

____ Optimistic, see difficulties as temporary, expect to overcome them and have things turn out well.

____ In a crisis, I calm myself and focus on taking useful actions.

____ Good at solving problems logically.

____ Can think up creative solutions to challenges. I trust my intuition.

____ Feel self-confident, enjoy healthy self-esteem, and have an attitude of professionalism about work.

____ Playful, find the humor, laugh at self, chuckle.

____ Curious, ask questions, want to know how things work, experiment.

____ Constantly learning from experience and from the experiences of others.

____ Very flexible. Feel comfortable with inner complexity (trusting and cautious, unselfish and selfish, optimistic and pessimistic, etc.).

____ Anticipate problems to avoid them and expect the unexpected.

____ Able to tolerate ambiguity and uncertainty about situations.

____ Good listener. Good empathy skills. "Read" people well. Can adapt to various personality styles. Non-judgmental (even with difficult people).

____ Able to recover emotionally from losses and setbacks. Can express feelings to others, let go of anger, overcome discouragement, and ask for help.

____ Very durable, keep on going during tough times. Independent spirit.

____ Have been made stronger and better by difficult experiences.

____ Convert misfortune into good fortune. Discover the unexpected benefit.

Adapted with permission from *The Survivor Personality* by Al Siebert, PhD.[48] For more detailed information, please visit The Resiliency Center's site and research articles: www.resiliencycenter.com

Self-Assessment

Scoring: How Resilient Are You?

75 or higher ....Very Resilient!
65-74..Better than most
55-64..Slow, but adequate
45-54..You're struggling
45 or under ....Seek help!

Interpretation

Highly resilient people display many similar qualities:

- Playful, childlike curiosity

- Constantly learn from experience

- Adapt quickly

- Have solid self-esteem and self-confidence

- Self-confidence in your reputation with yourself

- Have good friendships, loving relationships

- Express feelings honestly

- Expect things to work out well

- Read others with empathy

- Use intuition, creative hunches

- Defend self well

This self-assessment, scoring, and interpretation are all adapted with permission from *The Survivor Personality* by Al Siebert, PhD.[48] For more detailed information, please visit The Resiliency Center's site and research articles: www.resiliencycenter.com

How to Keep Yourself Motivated and Resilient

At first, it might seem like we have addressed this topic. But think about this: What's the difference between motivation and resiliency? There is a difference, and it's an important distinction.

- *Motivation* comes from a place of inspiration, purpose, enthusiasm, and internal desire.

- *Resiliency* is the fuel, spirit, hardiness and buoyancy that allows you to initiate action and see it through.

Can you see how a person might have the aspiration, but no fuel to drive it forward? Has this ever happened to you?

Have you had times when you became so focused on the operation, project, or task at hand that you worked late every night? That sort of sustained effort can drain your reserves. If you focus so much on workplace issues that your family begins to feel neglected, that's a clue that things are out of balance.

If you find yourself saying, "I know I really *should* _____, but I can't right now. I'm just too wiped out." for longer than a month or two at a time, that's a red flag that your reserves are dangerously low. It is critical to pay attention to your self-care and your personal energy management. You can be sure that your employees and colleagues will notice the difference when you take good care of yourself – and when you don't.

Stephen Covey writes about "sharpening the saw" as one of the *Seven Habits of Highly Effective People*. The idea here is that if the saw blade is dull, you will be working harder than you need to.

Take the time to sharpen the saw, and your work will go faster and easier.

Similarly, you know you have to fill up your gas tank to keep your car running. What are you doing to refuel *your* tank?

And what about oil changes? Do you take *yourself* in for a little extra service every few months or few thousand miles?

▶ When was your last big dose of fun and relaxation?

And finally, there's always the classic attitude question: Is the glass half-full or half-empty?

Try this. The next time you reach over to pick up your water bottle (or cup of coffee), take a quick attitude check. *What's your attitude like today?*

These metaphors help remind us that no matter how hard we work (or want to work), if we don't take time for self-care, we will soon be running on empty.

Now let's take this idea back to the workplace. It's important to your employees and peers that *you* stay motivated and resilient.

It's also important that you support *them* in staying resilient. This involves more than just approving vacation scheduling requests. We're talking about supporting your employees in sustaining their ability to take initiative, feel hopeful and confident, and enjoy contributing.

▶ What are some things you do now to help your employees stay resilient?

▶ What are some new ideas to keep yourself motivated and resilient?

It is important for everyone to attend to *all* aspects of their health—physical, mental and emotional. For leaders, it's even more important. You are a role model, like it or not. Lead with your actions.

Ideas for Sustaining the Momentum

As a leader, you know that different people have strengths during different stages of change or a project. Some are good at visioning; others are good at the details. Some are good at initiating, while others are good at follow-through. You also know that a key component to success, especially during lean times, is the ability to sustain the momentum.

Here are some ideas to help keep yourself and others motivated through the long-term life of a change or project, and during uncertain times.

- Stay connected with your peers and colleagues – bounce ideas off one another.

- Share motivational quotes. They are great reminders.

- Spend time with inspirational people – ask how they sustain their momentum.

- Create a zero tolerance culture in your workplace, which means no tolerance for chronic negativity or gossip. As you implement this change of culture, it is important to still allow concerns or complaints to be aired, and to differentiate between healthy and toxic negativity. This will increase trust, confidentiality and motivation, in addition to increasing the "direct communication" between two people. It's very productive!

- Assure employees that they can come to you for advice at any time, and give them permission to do that sooner than later—especially during lean times. Then listen non-defensively, deeply and supportively.

- Have regular check-in meetings with employees to generate strategies on how to address emergent issues.

- Search for books and other resources. There's a lot of useful information out there to help leaders lead. Use pertinent keywords to search the web. Or check out the latest offerings at your favorite bookseller. [If you need a place to start, go to www.marytmeyer.com/resources/ and scan the Recommended Reading list.]

▶ How will *you* sustain the momentum for yourself and your employees?

Resiliency Summary

Here are a few key points that you have learned in this chapter:

- Resiliency is the quality that helps us to endure the multiple simultaneous changes, and all the extra efforts that are required of us.

- Resiliency is what gives us the ability to sustain momentum during lean times.

- When leaders are able to stay resilient, they are better able to treat people with consideration. They have the ability to stay centered as new challenges arise, and to see the most feasible solution to those challenges.

- When leaders are resilient, they act as models for their employees to stay focused while moving forward.

What does resiliency have to do with leadership and motivation? Everything!

CHAPTER 11

ACTION PLAN AND APPLICATION

At the beginning of this book, you were presented with six objectives to accomplish:

1. Describe your leadership style during challenges and changes.
2. Explore several emerging leadership trends including Servant Leadership, Stewardship, LEAN Management, and Embracing Diversity.
3. Identify current issues in your team or organization.
4. Apply several strategies to motivate your employees.
5. Develop strategies to sustain momentum and resiliency.
6. Write and implement a short-term action plan to apply these concepts.

We have presented information on each of the topic areas, and provided you with the tools to accomplish those objectives.

Now, take a moment to reflect on whether or not you feel ready to move forward. Move forward to what? To start making improvements in the ways you lead and motivate your employees. Think about the learning highlights from this book.

▶ What actions will you take in the next two weeks to apply what you've learned? To be truly accountable, it's important for you to:

- Identify your strategy

- Develop an action plan with progressive steps to follow

- Name the person to whom you will be accountable

- Select a date when you will complete your action plan for each strategy.

Complete the action plan that follows. Two strategies have been added for you. You can add two more of your own.

Strategies	Action Steps	Who	When
Motivate my employees			
Sustain momentum and resiliency (for self or others)			

▶ What is your level of confidence in following through on your action plan?

Very Confident		On the Fence		Low Confidence
1	2	3	4	5

▶ If you rated yourself at 1 or 2, great. Go for it! Let me hear about your success stories! [www.marytmeyer.com]

▶ If you rated yourself at 3 or above, what could you do to boost your confidence?

Look back at the second page of Chapter 2 and the two challenges you selected. Compare your action plan with your initial strategies. What do you notice? Any similarities or differences? Were the initial issues you identified the same as the underlying causes that need to be resolved? Do you have any new strategies after reading this book?

Remember the comment about surveys that were completed and filed away in a drawer – and there was never any follow-up? (See Chapter 8 section on "Traditional vs. Strategic Innovation.") This is a similar juncture. Action plans are useful only when you create them and USE them! Move it off the paper and into motion… *Make it happen!*

If you need assistance and coaching support for developing your action plan or increasing your confidence, I encourage you to visit www.marytmeyer.com for helpful resources.

Closing Thoughts

Thank you for taking time to study the concepts presented in this book and reflect on your role as a leader. These are busy times, and often reflection time is a luxury. However, it is these moments of pause that lead to perspective and insight, which are both essential leadership traits.

In *Leadership and Motivation*, you learned what leadership is along with current practices and new trends. We have examined how employee motivation is enhanced by LEAN management, effective change management, embracing diversity, positive recognition, celebration, accountability, innovation and resiliency.

Always remember that, as a leader, people are watching you. They look to you for inspiration, for problem solving, and to hold people accountable. What attitudes and behaviors do you want to model for them? Be considerate. Speak respectfully, and be willing to give and receive feedback non-defensively.

Show managerial courage and *Step Up!*

Be clear about your personal mission every day! Why are you doing what you are doing? Go forth with passion, for the love of it! Make a difference each day. Build people up and develop leadership in others.

Look for the possibilities! Talk with your employees. Discuss various options for new ways of doing day-to-day activities. Help them to know clearly what is and is not negotiable.

Maintain your resiliency so you can be your best for the world.

"In the course of history, there comes a time when humanity is called to shift to a new level of consciousness, to reach a higher moral ground. A time when we have to shed our fear and give hope to each other. That time is now."
–WANGARI MAATHAI, 2004 NOBEL PEACE PRIZE WINNER

ABOUT THE AUTHOR

Mary T. Meyer, MS, has worked in Organization Development & Training for over twenty-five years, including eighteen years in public service. She was the Training Program Manager in local government for fourteen years, providing facilitation, consultation, training, and coaching to thousands of managers and supervisors, committees, project teams, task force members and departmental leaders. In the last two years, she has been a learning management system administrator and Training Manager serving the cities and counties throughout Oregon.

In addition to her public service, Mary has also worked in the healthcare, education, construction and banking industries. Her background includes a variety of roles and responsibilities: Supervisor, manager, operations manager, consultant, and business owner. She has advised city, county and state agencies as well as small businesses and international corporations.

Areas of expertise include leadership development, project management, teambuilding, managing change/transition, conflict resolution, process improvement, team problem-solving, operations management, strategic planning, succession planning and career development.

Mary holds an MS in Organization Development as well as a BA in Speech and Communication. She is a member of the Society for Human Resources Management (SHRM) and the American Society for Training and Development (ASTD). She is the owner of MTM Consulting, and enjoys life in Oregon. For more information, go to: www.marytmeyer.com.

BIBLIOGRAPHY AND REFERENCES

The author gratefully acknowledges permission to use quotations or passages from the sources listed below. Regarding reprint permission, diligent efforts were made to obtain permission to reprint selections from previously published works.

What is Leadership?
1. Warren Bennis, *On Becoming a Leader*. Revised edition (2003), Basic Books.
    Peter Drucker, *The Leader of the Future* [Foreward], Editors: Frances Hesselbein, Marshall Goldsmith, Richard Beckhard, (1996), Jossey-Bass.
    Collins English Dictionary, (1998), HarperCollins Publishers.
    Clark definition sourced from Clark, Don R., *Concepts of Leadership*, (2004)
    Peter Northouse, *Leadership: Theory and Practice*, 4th edition (2007), Sage Publishing.

Leadership vs. Management
2. Mary Anne Huard, Southwest Training Institute, http://www.swtinstitute.com/
3. David Straker, "Leadership vs. Management"
    See Also: *Changing Minds: in Detail*, 2nd edition (2010), Syque Press.

Principles of Leadership
4. Stephen R. Covey, *Principle-Centered Leadership*, 1st edition (September 1991), Simon & Schuster.
5. United States Army, *U.S. Army Principles of Leadership*, (1983).

Your Leadership Style
6. Hersey, P. and Blanchard, K. H. (1977), *Management of Organizational Behavior 3rd Edition—Utilizing Human Resources*, 3rd Edition (1977), Prentice Hall.
7. Leadership Style Assessment [Parts 1-4] are from the *Compendium of Questionnaires and Inventories* Volume II, by Sarah Cook, copyright © 2007. Used by permission of the publisher, HRD Press, Inc., Amherst, MA. (800)822-2801. www.hrdpress.com

Leadership in the Public Sector
8. Keith Malo, AchieveGlobal Research Manager, "Critical Crossroads: Developing Leaders in the Public Sector," (2003), AchieveGlobal, Inc. www.Achieveglobal.org

Emerging Trends in Leadership
9. Laura E. Bernstein, *Peer Today, Boss Tomorrow*, (2005), The WALK THE TALK Company. [© Laura E. Bernstein, used with permission.] www.WalktheTalk.com
See also: *Peer Today, Boss Tomorrow*[TM] training available from Sollah Interactive, LLC

LEAN Management
10. Description of LEAN Management excerpted with permission from the State of Oregon Employment Department LEAN Management Basics training.

Leading at a Higher Level
11. Ken Blanchard, Leading at a Higher Level, FT Press (2006), www.kenblanchardcompanies.com

Servant Leadership
12. Servant Leadership excerpts from the writings of Robert K. Greenleaf are reprinted by permission of the Greenleaf Center for Servant Leadership. © Robert K. Greenleaf Center, Inc. 2008.
13. Robert Bacal/Bacal & Associates, "*Servant Leadership*," © 2007-2010, http://work911.com/articles/

Stewardship
14. Peter Block, *Stewardship*, Berrett-Koehler Publishers (1993).

The Future of Leadership
Common themes were derived from multiple sources:
15. Ann Egros, PharmD., "Leadership Skills for 2020." http://zestnzen.com/
16. ibid.
17. ibid.
18. ibid.
19. Hernez-Broome, G. and Hughes, R.L., "Leadership Development: Past Present and Future," Human Resources Planning, Vol 27-1, pp 24-32, Human Resource Planning Society (2004). http://www.bpir.com/
20. Ann Egros, PharmD., "Leadership Skills for 2020." http://zestnzen.com/
21. Hernez-Broome, G. and Hughes, R.L., "Leadership Development: Past Present and Future," Human Resources Planning, Vol 27-1, pp 24-32, Human Resource Planning Society (2004). http://www.bpir.com/
22. Jim Carroll, "Future Trends," www.jimcarroll.com
23. ibid.
24. Friedman, Thomas, *The World is Flat*, Farrar, Straus & Giroux (2006)
25. Dale Allen, "In Our Right Minds", CD/DVD, Copyright © 2009 Dale Allen Productions, LLC., http://daleallenproductions.com/iorm_index.htm

What is Motivation?
26. Motivation defined: CliffNotes/Leadership Defined, http://www.cliffsnotes.com/study_guide/Leadership-Defined.topicArticleId-8944,articleId-8913.html#ixzz0wbk8FKUU

Positive Recognition
27. "Celebrate What's Right with the World," http://www.celebratewhatsright.com/. Copyright MMX Dewitt Jones.

Leading Through Change
28. William Bridges, *Transitions*, Da Capo Press. (2003, 2009) http://www.wmbridges.com/http://www.wmbridges.com/books/books.html
29. ibid.
30. ibid.
31. James M. Kouzes and Barry Z. Posner, *The Leadership Challenge*, (2007), Jossey Bass-Wiley & Sonsner.
32. ibid.

Embracing a Diverse Workforce
33. "Defining Multiculturalism," en.wikipedia.org/wiki/Multiculturalism
34. Dr. Caleb Rosado, University of Oregon Multicultural Strategic Plan, pg 15, (1996) http://vpsa.uoregon.edu/wp-content/uploads/2010/06/Strategic-Action-Plan-Report1.pdf
35. Howe, Neil, and William Strauss, *Millennials Rising*, Vintage Press (2000).

Holding People Accountable
36. Source unknown. *[If you have any information regarding original source of this little story, please contact us and we will update the reference in future editions.]*
37. Wikipedia/Recall election, http://en.wikipedia.org/wiki/Recall_election.
38. Dan Oestreich and Kathleen Ryan, *Driving Fear Out of the Workplace*, (1998), Jossey-Bass, http://unfoldingleadership.com/

Performance Management
39. Chuck Williams, *Effective Management*, (2011), Southwestern College Publishing.

Strategic Innovation
40. Soren Kaplan and Derrick Palmer, "A Framework for Strategic Innovation", (2007), Innovation Point, http://www.innovation-point.com/Strategic%20Innovation%20White%20Paper.pdf
41. ibid.
42. Business Performance Improvement Resource [BPIR], "Principles of Innovative Learning" (2010), http://www.bpir.com/
43. Soren Kaplan and Derrick Palmer, "A Framework for Strategic Innovation", (2007), Innovation Point, http://www.innovation-point.com/Strategic%20Innovation%20White%20Paper.pdf
44. 44. ibid.
45. 45. ibid.

What is Resiliency?

46. Al Siebert, Ph.D., *The Survivor Personality*, (1996), Practical Psychology Press, See also: "The Resiliency Manual for Federal Employees," (2007), http://www.resiliencycenter.com/.

47. Lisa Latin, "Live + Learn", (2011), http://lisalatin.com

48. Al Siebert, Ph.D, *The Survivor Personality*, (1996), Practical Psychology Press, www.resiliencycenter.com/

Supplemental Materials provided on the author's website at www.marytmeyer.com

Keith Malo [AchieveGlobal Research Manager], "Critical Crossroads: Developing Leaders in the Public Sector", (2003), AchieveGlobal, Inc. www.Achieveglobal.org

LEAN Management Glossary, State of Oregon Employment Department

Harry Woodward, Ph.D., "What Happens to People During Transition," from *Working Through Change* video and workbook, (1996).

Susan Fee, "Creative Ways to Motivate Your Employees", (2010). http://www.susanfee.com/coaching/tips/CreativeWaystoMotivateYourEmployees.htm

INDEX

Index

www.ingramcontent.com/pod-product-compliance
Lightning Source LLC
Chambersburg PA
CBHW080302180526

45167CB00006B/2638